ACCELERATING SUSTAINABLE DEVELOPMENT AFTER COVID-19

THE ROLE OF SDG BONDS

JULY 2021

ACGF
ASEAN CATALYTIC GREEN FINANCE FACILITY

ADB

Notes:
In this publication, "$" refers to United States dollars.
ADB recognizes "Hong Kong" and "Hongkong" as Hong Kong, China; "China" as the People's Republic of China; "Vietnam" as Viet Nam; "Korea, Dem. Rep." as the Democratic People's Republic of Korea; and "Russia" as the Russian Federation.

Cover design by Edith Creus.

On the cover: SDG bonds can serve as a mechanism to help accelerate much-needed financing in developing Asia, especially to address the impacts of the coronavirus disease (COVID-19) pandemic (photos by Gerhard Jörén, Zen Nuntawinyu, Aaron March, and Eric Sales for ADB).

Contents

Contents

Tables, Figures, and Boxes

Boxes

Foreword

The Asian Development Bank (ADB) estimates that Southeast Asia will require $210 billion per year between 2016 and 2030 to support investment in vital climate-compatible infrastructure. Even before the coronavirus disease (COVID-19) pandemic, infrastructure investment, particularly from private capital sources, was far below the levels needed, with the investment gap estimated at between 3.8% of gross domestic product (GDP) to 4.1% of GDP (when taking climate change into account) between 2016 and 2020 in some members of the Association of Southeast Asian Nations (ASEAN).

The pandemic has clearly highlighted the link between viruses and diseases such as COVID-19 and climate change, oceans acidification, and biodiversity loss, with the poor suffering the most in all cases. Moving ahead, we need to create pathways that provide for equitable economic growth and sustainable use of the planet's natural resources.

This clearly emphasizes the need for a renewed focus on achieving the 17 Sustainable Development Goals (SDGs) launched by the United Nations (UN) Agenda 2030, as the global blueprint to end poverty, protect our planet, and ensure prosperity. Along with inadequate health systems, the pandemic has also exposed a few other challenges such as lack of access to education, failure to reach clean water and sanitation targets, and inadequate food security. These are all development gaps that the SDGs are trying to address. After COVID-19, every developing country will need to reassess progress in achieving the SDGs for equitable growth, conservation of natural resources, and action to reduce the impact of climate change.

Achieving the SDGs was always a challenge even before the COVID-19 pandemic. In the face of constrained public resources, the lack of bankable SDG projects meant many developing countries could not mobilize the resources required from the private sector, given the inherent risks. The complexity of applying SDG indicators and frameworks at the project level has been another factor hindering progress toward the SDGs. COVID-19 has clearly highlighted the pressing need for accelerated efforts to plan and mobilize resources for the SDGs. While challenging, the pandemic does also offer a new opportunity for countries to mainstream SDGs into their recovery plans to build resilience to future crises.

As developing countries make funding plans using a combination of concessionary finance mechanisms along with traditional sources, new instruments are being explored to bring in extra funding while inculcating better practices and sustainability principles. This publication provides an overview of SDG bonds that may help in mobilizing the finance needed to meet the sustainability goals in developing Asia. Besides funding to accelerate SDGs, the bonds could also help monitor progress achieved on sustainability overall. SDG bonds could act as both an "enabler" and an "enforcer" to help countries make real progress toward their SDG goals and provide an opportunity for a wide range of investors to play their part in meeting the emerging global sustainability norms. As a potential addition to efforts to increase sustainable finance, the publication suggests structured or transition SDG Accelerator Bonds.

Since 2018, the Southeast Asia Department (SERD) of ADB, through its Innovation Hub, has been developing new de-risking mechanisms to mobilize capital for green projects and companies to help bridge the infrastructure investment gap in the region. These efforts resulted in the signing of an agreements with the World Economic Forum in November 2019 to accelerate the flow of public and private finance into sustainable infrastructure in Southeast Asia through an ASEAN hub for the Sustainable Development Investment Partnership (SDIP). This publication has been developed in close collaboration with the SDIP ASEAN Hub and experts from the private sector.

ADB will continue to play a key role in supporting ASEAN members to develop green and bankable infrastructure projects that will stimulate economic recovery and create jobs, while supporting the goals of the Paris Agreement. The knowledge that is presented here could also be a small input for the upcoming United Nations Conference on Climate Change (COP26) to be hosted by the United Kingdom in November 2021.

Ramesh Subramaniam
Director General, Southeast Asia Department
Asian Development Bank
Co-chair of the Sustainable Development Investment Partnership (SDIP) ASEAN Hub

Key Messages from Peer Reviewers

Terri Toyota, head of Sustainable Markets Group; member of the Executive Committee, World Economic Forum. Innovation in sustainable development financing mechanisms is crucial for achieving the Sustainable Development Goals (SDGs) by 2030 and here the Asian Development Bank (ADB) has again demonstrated its thought leadership in sustainable development financing. The Sustainable Development Investment Partnership is honored and delighted to have partnered with ADB on this initiative, to positively accelerate the pace of capital flowing to meet the SDGs.

Don Kanak, chair, Prudential Insurance Growth Markets; cochair, Sustainable Development Investment Partnership, ASEAN Hub Steering Group. ADB's leadership with partners to create the Association of Southeast Asian Nations (ASEAN) Catalytic Green Finance Facility and its introduction of innovative new concepts, like the SDG Accelerator Bond, can make a major contribution to mobilizing finance for sustainable infrastructure and development, which is key to ASEAN's post-COVID-19 recovery and to the overall attainment of the SDGs.

Sophie Kemkhadze, deputy resident representative, United Nations Development Programme (UNDP) Indonesia. Congratulations to ADB for its role in advancing SDG Bonds for accelerating sustainable development after the coronavirus disease (COVID-19) pandemic. The urgency and importance of financing SDGs during this Decade of Action cannot be underestimated. SDG Accelerator Bonds can be a way forward to a whole-of-society inclusive approach that ensures gender equality perspectives are infused at all levels as countries work toward achieving the SDGs. Through our Innovative Financing Lab, UNDP Indonesia works with ADB and partners to promote innovative solutions that bridge the gap in financing SDGs. Working together, we can drive capital to where it is most needed, including through the application of UNDP's SDG Impact Standards for Bonds, and seize the opportunity to create a more sustainable and inclusive recovery pathway.

Ephyro Amatong, commissioner, Philippines Securities Exchange Commission. "Accelerating Sustainable Development after COVID-19: The Role of SDG Bonds" recognizes the challenges associated with "thematic investing," which the ASEAN Standards for Green, Sustainable, and Social bonds are meant to address. SDG Accelerator Bonds are a critically important addition to the financial instrument "toolbox" available to issuers and investors: blending the concessional aspects of limited public funds with the vastly greater amounts of market-rate private investments—and allocating the risks accordingly—will enable ASEAN countries to transition their economies toward a more sustainable, inclusive and, ultimately resilient, future.

About the Authors

This publication was developed by a joint team at the Southeast Asia Department of the Asian Development Bank (ADB) in collaboration with the Sustainable Development Investment Partnership (SDIP) for the Association of Southeast Asian Nations (ASEAN) region of the World Economic Forum (WEF). The innovative finance hub team at ADB worked closely with the SDIP team in developing the concept as well as undertaking peer reviews of the concept. The SDIP was launched in 2015 to scale finance for the Sustainable Development Goals and overcome barriers to private investment in emerging and developing countries. ADB is supporting the SDIP in this approach to ASEAN through an SDIP ASEAN Hub for which ADB and WEF signed a cooperation agreement in 2019.

ADB Team members

This publication was prepared by an ADB team led by Anouj Mehta, unit head, Green and Innovative Finance and the ASEAN Catalytic Green Finance Facility. The team included consultants Delphine Constantin, Sean Crowley, Raghu Dharmapuri Tirumala, Shivcharn Dhillion, Karthik Iyer, and Marina Lopez Andrich, and benefited from the collaboration of Hung Nguyen, senior regional cooperation specialist, Sustainable Development and Climate Change Department, ADB.

SDIP Team Members

The publication was developed in collaboration with the SDIP for the ASEAN region of the World Economic Forum, represented by Nikki Kemp, ASEAN Hub director.

Acknowledgments

The lead team of authors for this publication acknowledges contributions from members of the Asian Development Bank (ADB), the Southeast Asia Innovation Hub and the ASEAN Catalytic Green Finance Facility team, including: Joven Balbosa (advisor), Alfredo Perdiguero (director), Raquel Tabanao (associate knowledge management officer), Camille Bautista-Laguda (ACGF consultant) and Luisa Victoria Cadiz-Andrion (ACGF consultant). Editing by Layla Amar. Design and layout by Edith Creus.

The team especially thanks Smita Luthra Nakhooda (ADB senior results management specialist). The team is grateful for the inputs from Amitabh Mehta (Indus Blue Consultants, United Kingdom).

Overall supervision was provided by Ramesh Subramaniam, director general, ADB Southeast Asia Department.

The team greatly benefited from the guidance and inputs provided by the following peer reviewers.

Peer Reviewers and Advisors

- Terri Toyota, head of Sustainable Markets Group and member of the Executive Committee, World Economic Forum

- Nikki Kemp, ASEAN Hub director, SDIP, World Economic Forum

- Don Kanak, chair, Prudential Insurance Growth Markets; co-chair, Sustainable Development Investment Partnership, ASEAN Hub Steering Group

- Sophie Kemkhadze, deputy resident representative, United Nations Development Programme (UNDP) Indonesia.

- Ephyro Amatong, commissioner, Philippines Securities Exchange Commission

- Sylvain Vanston, group head, Climate & Environment, AXA

- Jean-Pascal Asseman, managing director, Infrastructure, AXA

- Arnaud Maricourt, head, Fixed Income Strategy and EM Research, AXA

- Veronica Chau, partner and director, Sustainable Investing & Social Impact, Boston Consulting Group

- Amitabh Mehta, Indus Blue Consultants

- Fuat Savas, executive director, JPMorgan Chase & Co.

- Saravanan Santhanam, director, Capital Projects & Infrastructure, PwC

- Smita Luthra Nakhooda, senior results management specialist, Strategy, Policy, and Partnerships Department, ADB

Abbreviations

ACGF	ASEAN Catalytic Green Finance Facility
ACMF	ASEAN Capital Markets Forum
ADB	Asian Development Bank
ASEAN	Association of Southeast Asian Nations
ASEAN SBS	ASEAN Social Bond Standards
ASEAN SUS	ASEAN Sustainability Bond Standards
B, bn or bio	billion
Bps	basis points
CAD or CA$	Canadian dollar
CSR	corporate social responsibility
COP	Colombian peso
COVID-19	coronavirus disease
EIB	European Investment Bank
ESG	environmental, social, governance
EU	European Union
EUR or €	euro
GAVI	Global Alliance for Vaccines and Immunization
GBP or £ pound sterling	British pound
KPI	key performance indicator
IADB	Inter-American Development Bank
ICMA	International Capital Market Association
ICMA GBP	ICMA Green Bond Principles
ICMA SBP	ICMA Social Bond Principles
IFFI	GAVI's International Finance Facility for Immunization
M, mn or mio	million

Mex$	Mexican peso
p.a.	per annum (per year)
SAB	SDG accelerator bond
SAI	Statement of Additional Information
SDG	Sustainable Development Goal
SDIP	Sustainable Development Investment Partnership
SEC	Securities and Exchange Commission (United States)
SERD	Southeast Asia Department (ADB)
SLL	Sustainability-Linked Loan
SSA	sovereigns, supranationals and agencies
SRI	socially responsible investing
UN	United Nations
US or U.S.	United States
USD or US$ or $	United States dollar
Yen or ¥	Japanese yen
WEF	World Economic Forum

GMS Kunming–Haiphong Transport Corridor. Noi Bai–Lao Cai Highway Project in Viet Nam. (photo by ADB).

1 Overview

While public finance is core to the implementation of the United Nations (UN) Sustainable Development Goals (SDGs), capital markets likewise plays a key role. This publication provides an overview of how bonds that align with the SDGs, or SDG bonds, can serve as a mechanism to accelerate the scale of finance needed to meet the sustainability goals of countries in developing Asia. The publication presents current approaches that are being adopted, along with the challenges to a wider issuance of SDG bonds. It subsequently sets out a proposal for a specific type of SDG bond that could accelerate the required momentum, especially after the massive impact of the coronavirus disease (COVID-19) crisis.

A. The COVID-19 Factor

The importance of development that provides not just equitable economic growth, but also sustainable use of the planet's natural resources, has perhaps never been more in focus than at this time of the COVID-19 pandemic. With over 175 million confirmed cases and over 3.8 million deaths worldwide (per the World Health Organization, 15 June 2021), governments are scrambling to spend funds on protecting incomes and providing urgent medical care to citizens. This is much needed, given International Labour Organization (ILO) early estimates that 305 million full-time jobs would be lost affecting 1.6 billion people in the informal sector, which have proved higher than originally forecasted with equivalent to 495 million full-time jobs lost globally only in the second quarter of the year.[1] The United Nations Educational, Scientific and Cultural

---

[1]   ILO. 2020. *ILO: As Job Losses Escalate, Nearly Half of Global Workforce at Risk of Losing Livelihoods.* 29 April; ILO. 2020. *COVID-19 Leads to Massive Labour Income Losses Worldwide.* 23 September.

Organization (UNESCO) estimates that 1.5 billion students or 52% of the world's student population are or have been affected by the pandemic.[2] The pandemic has also brought out sharply the huge unmet needs of the poorest and most vulnerable people in areas like healthcare, sanitation, water supply, affordable transport, and housing. Links are also being made between the emergence of viruses and diseases such as COVID-19 and climate change, ocean acidification, and biodiversity loss.[3]

B. A Renewed Focus on the SDGs

The year 2020 started the Decade for Action on achieving the 17 SDGs launched by the UN Agenda 2030. The 17 goals are the global blueprint to end poverty, protect our planet, and ensure prosperity. Prior to COVID-19, the Global Commission on the Economy and Climate had concluded that strong climate action has the potential to generate over 65 million new low-carbon jobs by 2030, deliver at least $26 trillion in net global economic benefits, and avoid 700,000 premature deaths from air pollution.[4] The Global Commission on Adaptation estimated that investing $1.8 trillion globally from 2020 to 2030 in resilience building measures could generate $7.1 trillion in total new benefits.[5] COVID-19 has served as a clear sign that a renewed focus on the SDGs is overdue. Aside from the weakness of health systems, the pandemic also exposes how far we are from achieving many of the SDGs, including the lack of education facilities, inadequate clean water and sanitation, and crises in poverty and food security. The World Bank estimates that COVID-19 will push an additional 71 million people into poverty in its baseline scenario and up to 100 million people in its downside scenario.[6]

Every developing country needs to renew its commitment to achieving the SDGs for equitable growth, conservation of natural resources, and reducing the impact of climate change, which is a cross-cutting theme across almost all the SDGs.[7] This is strongly supported by the UN, multilateral development banks (MDBs), and other organizations working for global sustainable development.[8] During the UN SG High-Level Meeting on Financing for Development in the Era of COVID-19 and Beyond on 8 September 2020, 50 heads of state affirmed their commitment to finding new ways to mobilize finance for the SDGs as a way out of the crisis.[9]

Challenges and Solutions

Achieving the SDGs was proving a challenge for many developing countries before COVID-19 for the following reasons:

(i) **Massive amounts of financing needed.** The UN has estimated that annual financing of $5 trillion to $7 trillion globally will be needed to meet the SDGs.[10]

---

[2] United Nations Educational, Scientific and Cultural Organization (UNESCO). *Global Education Coalition for COVID-19 Response.*

[3] United Nations Framework Convention on Climate Change (UNFCCC). 2017. *Human Health and Adaptation: Understanding Climate Impacts on Health and Opportunities for Action.* Synthesis Report by the Secretariat. Subsidiary Body for Scientific and Technological Advice 46th Session. Bonn. 8–18 May; Government of the United States, Department of Commerce, National Oceanic and Atmospheric Administration. 2020. Ocean Acidification.

[4] The Global Commission on the Economy and Climate. 2018. *Unlocking the Inclusive Growth Story of the 21st Century: Accelerating Climate Action in Urgent Times. Key Findings and Executive Summary.*

[5] Global Commission on Adaptation. 2019. *Adapt Now: A Global Call for Leadership on Climate Resilience.* 13 September.

[6] D. G. Mahler et al. 2020. "Updated Estimates of the Impact of COVID-19 on Global Poverty." Data Blog. *World Bank Blog.* 8 June.

[7] Climate Bonds Initiative. 2018. Green Bonds as a Bridge to the SDGs. June.

[8] B. Susantono, A. Alisjahbana, and K. Wignaraja. 2020. *A Determined Path to SDGs in 2030, Despite COVID-19 Pandemic.* ADB. 20 August.

[9] UN. 2020. *High-Level Event on Financing for Development in the Era of COVID-19 and Beyond. Initiative on Financing for Development in the Era of COVID-19 and Beyond.*

[10] United Nations Conference on Trade and Development (UNCTAD). 2014. *World Investment Report. Investing in the SDGs: An Action Plan.* New York: United Nations.

(ii) **Limited integration.** The limited integration of the SDGs into infrastructure planning due to systemic lack of capacity, political will, and other challenges results in a lack of substantial national SDG project pipelines.

(iii) **Substantial private finance required.** The private finance share required is over 50% in most countries and made worse because government budgets have been diverted to COVID-19 emergency relief and recovery work.

(iv) **Countries' limited capacity.** The limited capacity in countries to create bankable SDG projects that can attract commercial lending and/or private capital.

(v) **Complexity of applying SDG indicators and frameworks at project levels.** This results in deviations or inaccuracies which expose issuers to potential legal action, reputational damage, and eventual economic costs.

Solutions to the above challenges, especially those that can be applied to project development, for those that promote the SDGs and are bankable enough to attract private capital at scale, require institutional capacity building, along with national project funds. Several countries are undertaking such measures.

> "As attention shifts from the immediate health and human effects of the pandemic to addressing its social and economic effects, governments and societies face unprecedented policy, regulatory, and fiscal choices. The SDGs—a commitment to eradicate poverty and achieve sustainable development globally by 2030— can serve as a beacon in these turbulent times"
>
> **Armida Salsiah Alisjahbana, United Nations (UN) Under-Secretary-General and Executive Secretary of the Economic and Social Commission for Asia and the Pacific; Kanni Wignaraja, UN Assistant Secretary-General and Director for Asia and the Pacific, United Nations Development Programme; and Bambang Susantono, Asian Development Bank Vice-President for Knowledge Management and Sustainable Development.**

In this context, the application of UN standards and frameworks for the SDGs is required at national level. Clear and practical national SDG frameworks that can easily be applied to measure and monitor project and country SDG impacts and achievements can feed into a country's investment and development planning. This can help create appropriate pipelines of projects that promote the SDGs. The UN Global Indicator Framework, with 231 unique indicators, can be applied in a local or national context to support governments and MDBs.[11] Additionally, the Sustainable Development Investment Partnership (SDIP) Country Financing Roadmap initiative supports countries in public and private sector stakeholder engagement to produce national development financing road maps with integrated SDG outcomes.[12]

In terms of performance, the UN Sustainable Development Solutions Network, in collaboration with Bertelsmann Stiftung and Cambridge University Press, have created a prototype index that has been measuring annual country progress toward the 17 SDGs since 2015, showing their relative position between the worst and the best outcomes. The 2020 SDG index ranks 166 countries, as shown in Figure 1, and concludes that East, South, and Southeast Asia are the regions that have progressed most on the SDG Index since the adoption of the goals in 2015, based on the results of its 2020 SDG dashboard, as shown in Figure 2.[13]

---

[11] UN. SDG Indicators.

[12] SDIP. Country Financing Roadmaps.

[13] J. Sachs et al. 2020. *The Sustainable Development Report 2020: Sustainable Development Goals and COVID-19.* Cambridge: Cambridge University Press. 30 June.

Figure 1: The 2020 SDG Index Scores

Rank	Country	Score	Rank	Country	Score
1	Sweden	84.7	43	Greece	74.3
2	Denmark	84.6	44	Luxembourg	74.3
3	Finland	83.8	45	Uruguay	74.3
4	France	81.1	46	Ecuador	74.3
5	Germany	80.8	47	Ukraine	74.2
6	Norway	80.8	48	China	73.9
7	Austria	80.7	49	Vietnam	73.8
8	Czech Republic	80.6	50	Bosnia and Herzegovina	73.5
9	Netherlands	80.4	51	Argentina	73.2
10	Estonia	80.1	52	Kyrgyz Republic	73.0
11	Belgium	80.0	53	Brazil	72.7
12	Slovenia	79.8	54	Azerbaijan	72.6
13	United Kingdom	79.8	55	Cuba	72.6
14	Ireland	79.4	56	Algeria	72.3
15	Switzerland	79.4	57	Russian Federation	71.9
16	New Zealand	79.2	58	Georgia	71.9
17	Japan	79.2	59	Iran, Islamic Rep.	71.8
18	Belarus	78.8	60	Malaysia	71.8
19	Croatia	78.4	61	Peru	71.8
20	Korea, Rep.	78.3	62	North Macedonia	71.4
21	Canada	78.2	63	Tunisia	71.4
22	Spain	78.1	64	Morocco	71.3
23	Poland	78.1	65	Kazakhstan	71.1
24	Latvia	77.7	66	Uzbekistan	71.0
25	Portugal	77.6	67	Colombia	70.9
26	Iceland	77.5	68	Albania	70.8
27	Slovak Republic	77.5	69	Mexico	70.4
28	Chile	77.4	70	Turkey	70.3
29	Hungary	77.3	71	United Arab Emirates	70.3
30	Italy	77.0	72	Montenegro	70.2
31	United States	76.4	73	Dominican Republic	70.2
32	Malta	76.0	74	Fiji	69.9
33	Serbia	75.2	75	Armenia	69.9
34	Cyprus	75.2	76	Oman	69.7
35	Costa Rica	75.1	77	El Salvador	69.6
36	Lithuania	75.0	78	Tajikistan	69.4
37	Australia	74.9	79	Bolivia	69.3
38	Romania	74.8	80	Bhutan	69.3
39	Bulgaria	74.8	81	Panama	69.2
40	Israel	74.6	82	Bahrain	68.8
41	Thailand	74.5	83	Egypt, Arab Rep.	68.8
42	Moldova	74.4	84	Jamaica	68.7

continued on next page

Figure 1 continued

Rank	Country	Score
85	Nicaragua	68.7
86	Suriname	68.4
87	Barbados	68.3
88	Brunei Darussalam	68.2
89	Jordan	68.1
90	Paraguay	67.7
91	Maldives	67.6
92	Cabo Verde	67.2
93	Singapore	67.0
94	Sri Lanka	66.9
95	Lebanon	66.7
96	Nepal	65.9
97	Saudi Arabia	65.8
98	Trinidad and Tobago	65.8
99	Philippines	65.5
100	Ghana	65.4
101	Indonesia	65.3
102	Belize	65.1
103	Qatar	64.7
104	Myanmar	64.6
105	Honduras	64.4
106	Cambodia	64.4
107	Mongolia	64.0
108	Mauritius	63.8
109	Bangladesh	63.5
110	South Africa	63.4
111	Gabon	63.4
112	Kuwait	63.1
113	Iraq	63.1
114	Turkmenistan	63.0
115	São Tomé and Príncipe	62.6
116	Lao PDR	62.1
117	India	61.9
118	Venezuela, RB	61.7
119	Namibia	61.6
120	Guatemala	61.5
121	Botswana	61.5
122	Vanuatu	60.9
123	Kenya	60.2
124	Guyana	59.7
125	Zimbabwe	59.5

Rank	Country	Score
126	Syrian Arab Republic	59.3
127	Senegal	58.3
128	Côte d'Ivoire	57.9
129	The Gambia	57.9
130	Mauritania	57.7
131	Tanzania	56.6
132	Rwanda	56.6
133	Cameroon	56.5
134	Pakistan	56.2
135	Congo, Rep.	55.2
136	Ethiopia	55.2
137	Burkina Faso	55.2
138	Djibouti	54.6
139	Afghanistan	54.2
140	Mozambique	54.1
141	Lesotho	54.0
142	Uganda	53.5
143	Burundi	53.5
144	Eswatini	53.4
145	Benin	53.3
146	Comoros	53.1
147	Togo	52.7
148	Zambia	52.7
149	Angola	52.6
150	Guinea	52.5
151	Yemen, Rep.	52.3
152	Malawi	52.2
153	Sierra Leone	51.9
154	Haiti	51.7
155	Papua New Guinea	51.7
156	Mali	51.4
157	Niger	50.1
158	Dem. Rep. Congo	49.7
159	Sudan	49.6
160	Nigeria	49.3
161	Madagascar	49.1
162	Liberia	47.1
163	Somalia	46.2
164	Chad	43.8
165	South Sudan	43.7
166	Central African Republic	38.5

SDG = Sustainable Development Goal.
Source: Sustainable Development Report 2020.

Figure 2: SDG Levels and Trends for East, South, and Southeast Asia, 2020

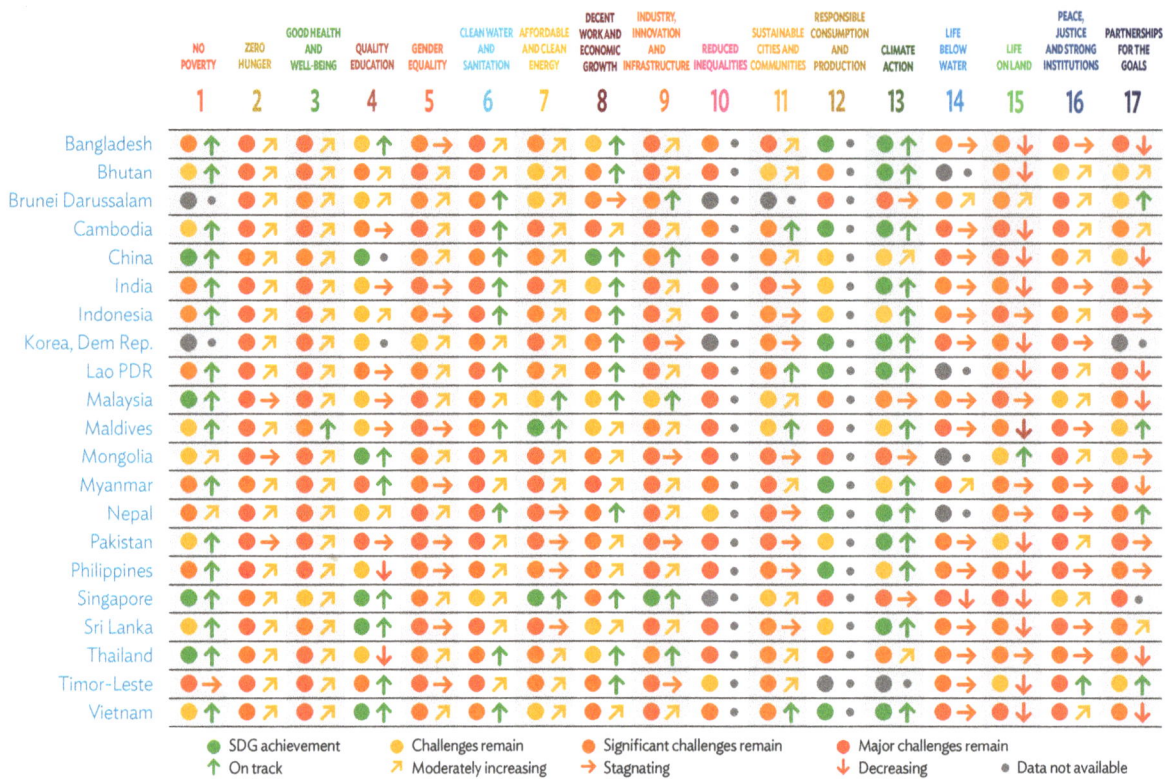

	1 NO POVERTY	2 ZERO HUNGER	3 GOOD HEALTH AND WELL-BEING	4 QUALITY EDUCATION	5 GENDER EQUALITY	6 CLEAN WATER AND SANITATION	7 AFFORDABLE AND CLEAN ENERGY	8 DECENT WORK AND ECONOMIC GROWTH	9 INDUSTRY, INNOVATION AND INFRASTRUCTURE	10 REDUCED INEQUALITIES	11 SUSTAINABLE CITIES AND COMMUNITIES	12 RESPONSIBLE CONSUMPTION AND PRODUCTION	13 CLIMATE ACTION	14 LIFE BELOW WATER	15 LIFE ON LAND	16 PEACE, JUSTICE AND STRONG INSTITUTIONS	17 PARTNERSHIPS FOR THE GOALS
Bangladesh																	
Bhutan																	
Brunei Darussalam																	
Cambodia																	
China																	
India																	
Indonesia																	
Korea, Dem Rep.																	
Lao PDR																	
Malaysia																	
Maldives																	
Mongolia																	
Myanmar																	
Nepal																	
Pakistan																	
Philippines																	
Singapore																	
Sri Lanka																	
Thailand																	
Timor-Leste																	
Vietnam																	

Legend:
- ● SDG achievement
- ● Challenges remain
- ● Significant challenges remain
- ● Major challenges remain
- ↑ On track
- ↗ Moderately increasing
- → Stagnating
- ↓ Decreasing
- • Data not available

Source: Sustainable Development Report 2020.

Looking into Southeast Asia, the region has made significant progress in the recent years toward achieving the SDGs, with increasing access to diverse channels of public and private, domestic and international financial options. This trajectory presents a potential opportunity if the funds can be judiciously raised and directed toward SDG projects. Reflecting the different opportunities and constraints across different countries, diversity of the financing landscape across the ASEAN region, CLMV countries (Cambodia, Lao PDR, Myanmar, and Viet Nam) and ASEAN-5 is presented in the Figure 3. While the aggregate resource growth is encouraging, the financial flows are limited, and are growing at a slower pace in a few countries. Domestic public finance continue to be the largest source across the region. The rise of domestic private finance is visible in all countries with 32% in the ASEAN, 22% in CLMV countries, and 35% in ASEAN-5.[14]

---

[14] United Nations Development Programme. 2017. *Financing the Sustainable Development Goals in ASEAN.* 16 November.

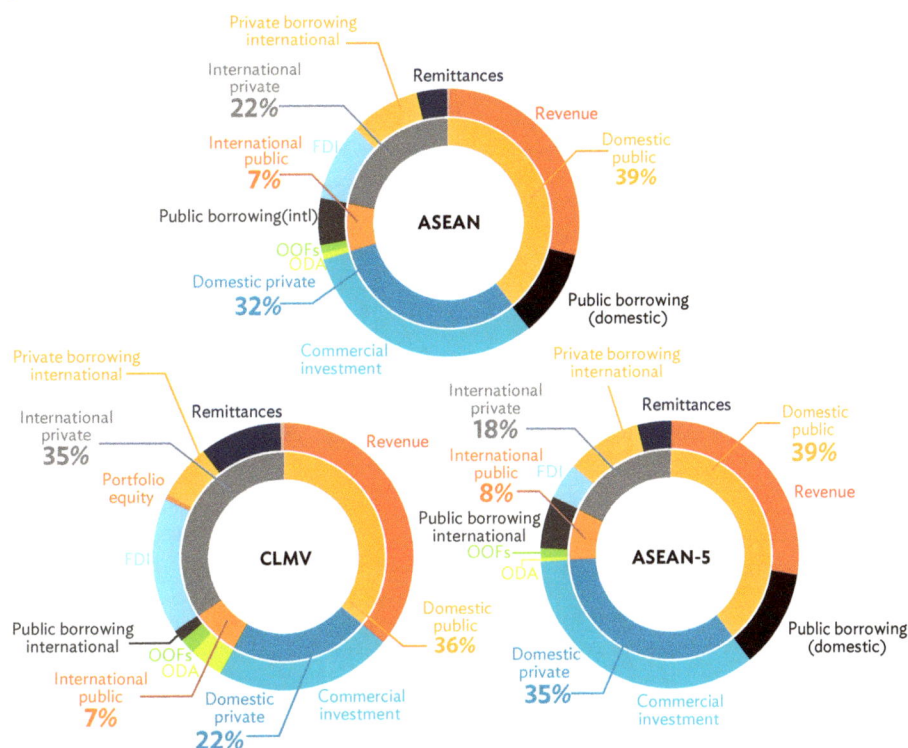

Figure 3: Finance Landscape for Sustainable Development in Southeast Asia

CLMV = Cambodia, Lao People's Democratic Republic, Myanmar, and Viet Nam; ASEAN = Association of Southeast Asian Nations; ASEAN-5 countries = Indonesia, Malaysia, the Philippines, Singapore, and Thailand; FDI = foreign direct investment, ODA = official development assistance, OOF = Other official flows.
Source: United Nations Development Programme. 2017. Financing the Sustainable Development Goals in ASEAN.

C. ADB's Approach to the SDGs

The Asian Development Bank (ADB) is committed that its investments must meet the highest standards of sustainable development and deliver results that help its member countries realize the vision set out in Strategy 2030. Toward this objective, ADB is increasingly embedding the SDGs across its planning and reporting mechanisms, including in the templates for reports and recommendations of the president for project approvals, country partnership strategies and regional partnership strategies. ADB's approach to the increased achievement of SDG-aligned outcomes from its projects, including in context of COVID-19 recovery support, span across a holistic gamut of engagement ranging from alignment of key planning and reporting mechanisms, initiatives that support member country actions, improved operational support to help the member countries accelerate on SDG implementation, and tracking country SDG progress in order to measure the SDG results.

ADB is the first MDB to institute a classification system that attempts to capture the amount of financing attributable to specific SDGs and targets, and to triangulate the SDG targets proposed by this input-driven tagging method with SDG targets related to indicators in project design and monitoring frameworks. ADB proposes to adapt and refine its approach to ensure consistency with evolving MDB practice and other development practice such as guidance from the Organisation for Economic Co-operation and Development on linking projects reported as Total Official Support for Sustainable Development.[15]

---

[15] ADB. 2021. *ADB's Support for the Sustainable Development Goals: Enabling the 2030 Agenda for Sustainable Development through Strategy 2030*. Manila.

ADB's support to implementation of SDGs in the member countries is organized around the themes anchored in the 2030 Agenda for Sustainable Development and the Addis Ababa Action Agenda on financing for development: people, planet, prosperity, and sustainable infrastructure, as shown in Figure 4.[16]

There is broad recognition that public finance alone cannot meet the financing needs of the agenda, and that mobilizing finance from diverse sources, particularly the private sector, will be vital to achieve the SDGs.[17] ADB is promoting the critical role of finance, knowledge, capacity building support, and technology in realizing sustainable development aspirations by being a catalyzer of finance for development, provider of knowledge, convenor of partnerships, and promoter of innovative integrated solutions.

Figure 4: ADB Support to SDGs in 2019

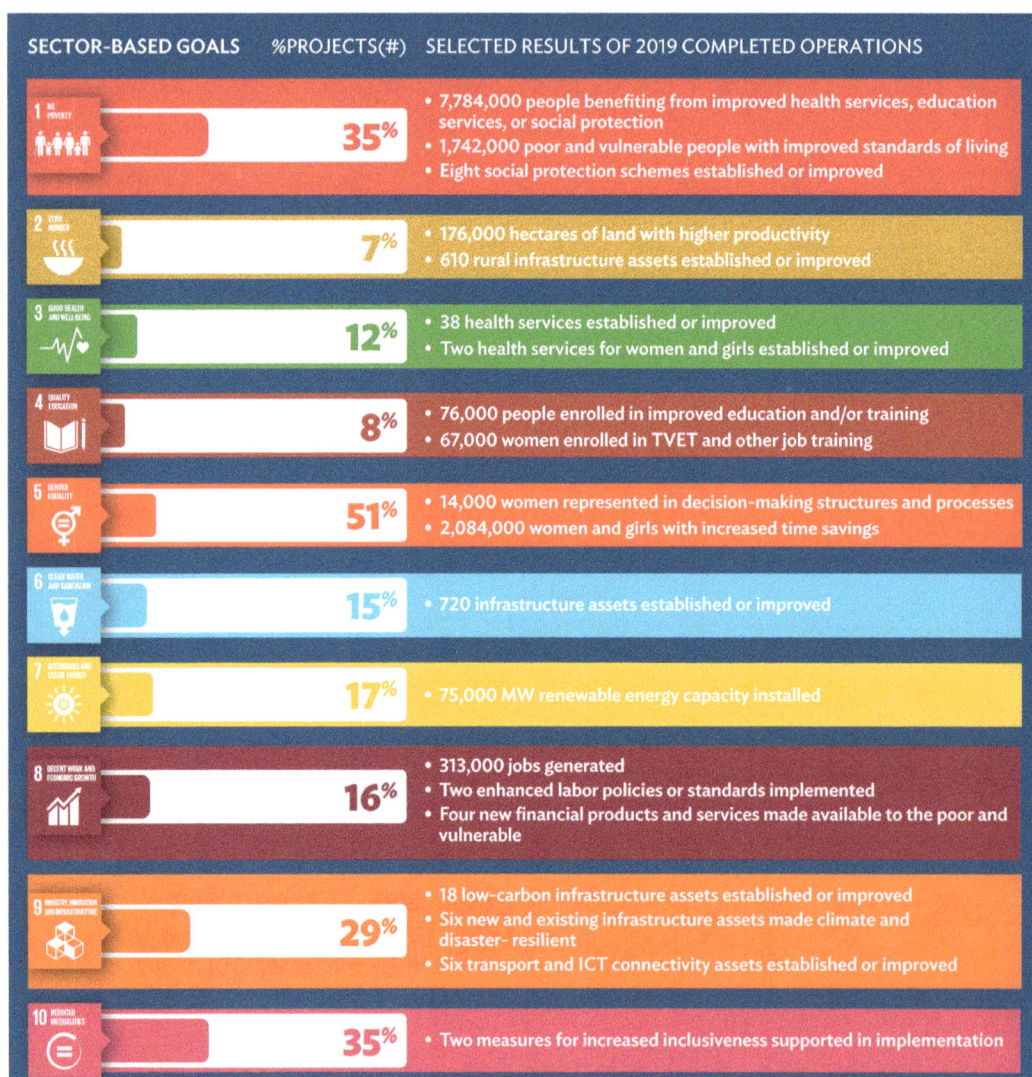

SECTOR-BASED GOALS	%PROJECTS(#)	SELECTED RESULTS OF 2019 COMPLETED OPERATIONS
1 NO POVERTY	35%	• 7,784,000 people benefiting from improved health services, education services, or social protection • 1,742,000 poor and vulnerable people with improved standards of living • Eight social protection schemes established or improved
2 ZERO HUNGER	7%	• 176,000 hectares of land with higher productivity • 610 rural infrastructure assets established or improved
3 GOOD HEALTH AND WELL-BEING	12%	• 38 health services established or improved • Two health services for women and girls established or improved
4 QUALITY EDUCATION	8%	• 76,000 people enrolled in improved education and/or training • 67,000 women enrolled in TVET and other job training
5 GENDER EQUALITY	51%	• 14,000 women represented in decision-making structures and processes • 2,084,000 women and girls with increased time savings
6 CLEAN WATER AND SANITATION	15%	• 720 infrastructure assets established or improved
7 AFFORDABLE AND CLEAN ENERGY	17%	• 75,000 MW renewable energy capacity installed
8 DECENT WORK AND ECONOMIC GROWTH	16%	• 313,000 jobs generated • Two enhanced labor policies or standards implemented • Four new financial products and services made available to the poor and vulnerable
9 INDUSTRY, INNOVATION AND INFRASTRUCTURE	29%	• 18 low-carbon infrastructure assets established or improved • Six new and existing infrastructure assets made climate and disaster-resilient • Six transport and ICT connectivity assets established or improved
10 REDUCED INEQUALITIES	35%	• Two measures for increased inclusiveness supported in implementation

continued on next page

---

[16] ADB. 2021. *ADB's Support for the Sustainable Development Goals: Enabling the 2030 Agenda for Sustainable Development through Strategy 2030*. Manila; ADB. 2020. *2019 Development Effectiveness Review: Scorecard and Related Information*. Manila; ADB. 2018. *Strategy 2030: Achieving a Prosperous, Inclusive, Resilient, and Sustainable Asia and the Pacific*. Manila.

[17] ADB. 2017. *Meeting Asia's Infrastructure Needs*. Manila.

Figure 4 *continued*

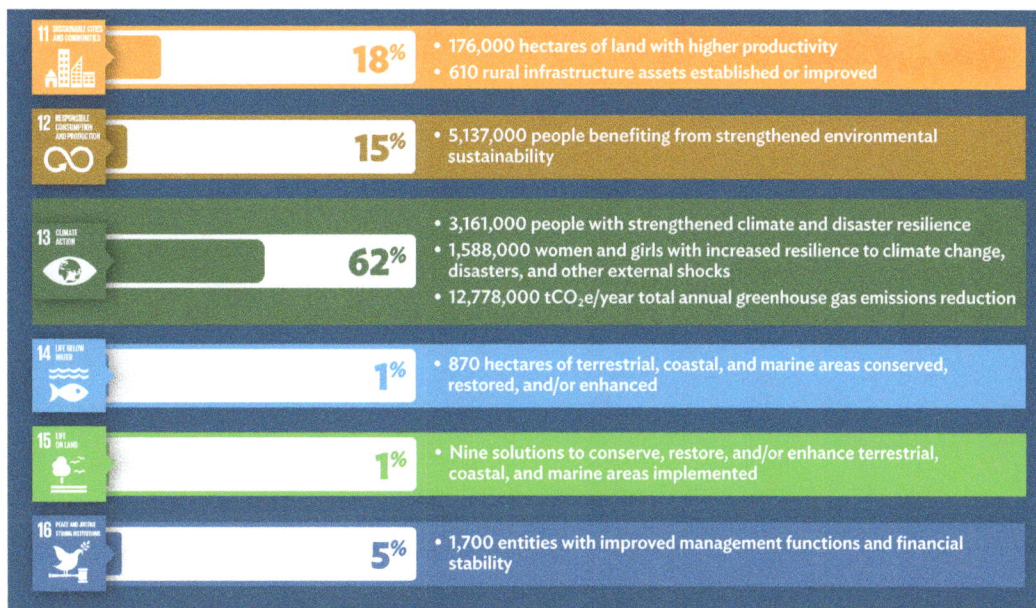

SDG	%	Outcomes
11 Sustainable Cities and Communities	18%	• 176,000 hectares of land with higher productivity • 610 rural infrastructure assets established or improved
12 Responsible Consumption and Production	15%	• 5,137,000 people benefiting from strengthened environmental sustainability
13 Climate Action	62%	• 3,161,000 people with strengthened climate and disaster resilience • 1,588,000 women and girls with increased resilience to climate change, disasters, and other external shocks • 12,778,000 tCO$_2$e/year total annual greenhouse gas emissions reduction
14 Life Below Water	1%	• 870 hectares of terrestrial, coastal, and marine areas conserved, restored, and/or enhanced
15 Life on Land	1%	• Nine solutions to conserve, restore, and/or enhance terrestrial, coastal, and marine areas implemented
16 Peace and Justice Strong Institutions	5%	• 1,700 entities with improved management functions and financial stability

ICT = information and communication technology, MW = megawatt, tCO$_2$e = tons of carbon dioxide equivalent, TVET = technical and vocational education and training.

Source: Asian Development Bank.

D. SDG Bonds Could Provide Momentum for SDG Financing

Since 2015, the growth of environmental, social, and governance (ESG), sustainable, and social bonds, have taken the thematic bond universe even further. The COVID-19 pandemic, the incidence of zoonotic disease crossing the animal and human divide, and its impacts on wider socioeconomic factors, has made more evident the need for a renewed focus on biodiversity, natural capital, and their interdependence with human development. As countries configure their funding plans using a combination of concessionary financing mechanisms from traditional funding sources, newer instruments are being explored to create funding additionality while inculcating more sustainable practices. According to Refinitiv, $275 billion of new financing was raised on capital markets during the first half of 2020, including sustainability bonds ($194.5 billion, up 47% from the same period in 2019), syndicated loans ($79.1 billion, a 2% decline compared to the first half of 2019), and equity capital ($4 billion, a 21% decline from the same period in 2019) issuance tied to sustainable outcomes. By region, Europe remains the main borrower of overall sustainable lending during the first half of 2020, representing 63% of total borrowing and 46% of the sustainable bonds market in the same period, as shown in Figure 5.[18]

Research done by the Climate Bonds Initiative (CBI) shows that green, social, and sustainability bonds almost doubled in 2020, with $700 billion worth of issuances. In 2020, green bonds remained the dominant theme. Social and sustainability financing peaked in early 2020 due to the pandemic, with social financing growing to over 10 times 2019 levels and sustainability financing rising to as much as 2.3 times the previous year's volume

---

[18] Refinitiv 2020. *Sustainable Finance Review First Half 2020.*

Figure 5: Sustainable Bonds in the First Half of 2020, by Region

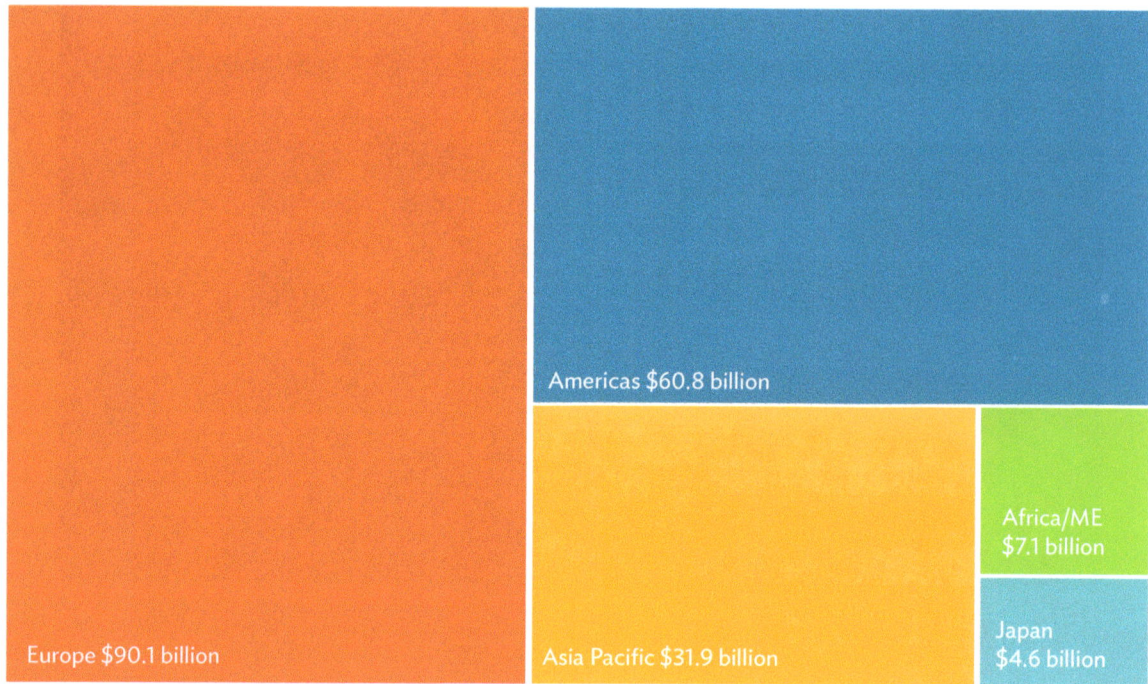

Americas $60.8 billion

Africa/ME $7.1 billion

Japan $4.6 billion

Europe $90.1 billion

Asia Pacific $31.9 billion

ME = Middle East.
Source: Refinitiv 2020. Sustainable Finance Review First Half 2020.

Figure 6: Green, Social, and Sustainability Bond Market

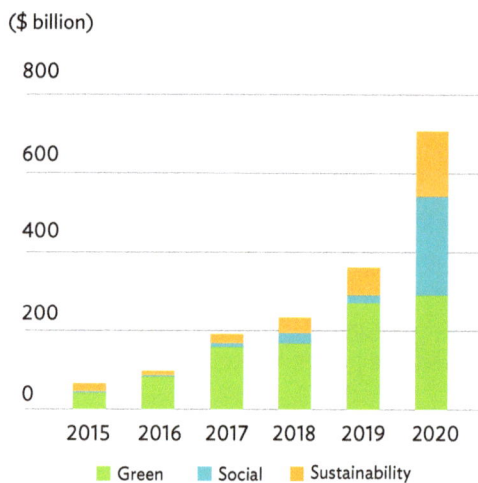

($ billion)

Green   Social   Sustainability

Source: Refinitiv 2020. Sustainable Finance Review First Half 2020.

Figure 7: Evolution of Green, Social, and Sustainability Bonds in 2020

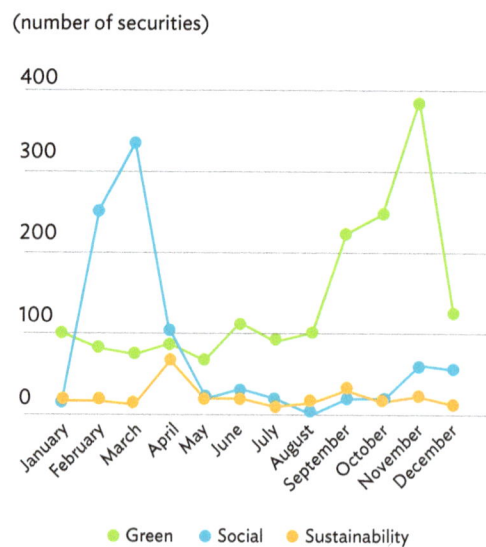

(number of securities)

Green   Social   Sustainability

Source: Climate Bonds Initiative. 2021. *Sustainable Debt: Global State of the Market 2020*. April.

(Figure 6). These levels settled toward the end of the year (Figures 7).[19] Looking into Southeast Asia, the overall issuance of green, social, and sustainable bonds and loans reached a record high of $12.1 billion in 2020, up slightly from the $11.5 billion issued in 2019, with Singapore, Thailand, and Indonesia leading the issuances in the region (Figure 8).[20]

Figure 8: Green, Social, and Sustainability Issuances in Southeast Asia, by Country

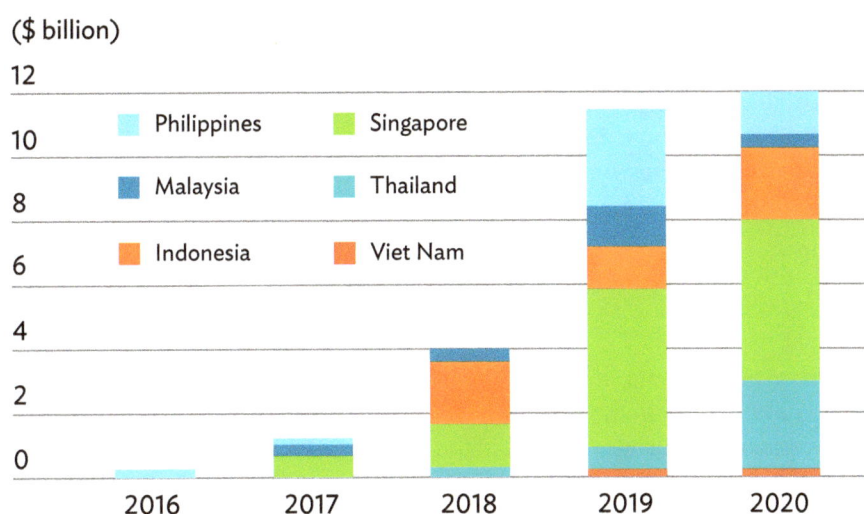

Source: Climate Bonds Initiative. 2021. *ASEAN Sustainable Finance State of the Market 2020*. April.

Anecdotal evidence as well as some recent research are leaning towards green bonds offering lower yields due to the investors being willing to accept lower returns to hold bonds identified as socially responsible or green. Based on 54 green bonds in the sample, a study reports strong evidence in support of green as 26 out of 33 bonds pr ice on curves or with a "greenium," defined as the higher price or premium that investors are willing to pay for bonds with green benefits.[21] Debate, however, continues on whether that higher price or premium investors are ready to pay (therefore the lower cost of capital that issuers pay) is a function of demand vs. supply rather than an actual appetite to forfeit returns in favour of impact.

As the impact of climate change become more acute, green bonds will continue to grow as a means of funding the response. Municipalities and cities should embrace them as a cheaper alternative and get access to a new breed of investors.

According to Refinitiv, the sustainable finance sector continued to grow during the first quarter of 2021. It showed double the growth against the same quarter in 2020 and raised $286.5 billions raised, with green bonds quadrupling from Q1 2020 to Q1 2021 to reach an all-time quarterly record of $131.3 billion. For the same quarter, sustainable equity transactions doubled while mergers and acquisitions in the sustainable space quadrupled year–on–year.[22]

---

[19] CBI. 2021. *Sustainable Debt: Global State of the Market 2020*. April.
[20] CBI. 2021. *ASEAN Sustainable Finance State of the Market 2020*. April.
[21] CBI. 2021. *Green Bond Pricing in the Primary Market: July-December 2020*. March.
[22] M. Toole. 2021. Sustainable Finance Continues Surge in Q1. *Refinitiv*. 23 April.

Increasingly, companies are embedding SDG frameworks into their business models and viewing SDG bonds as a financial instrument that could offer a flexible way to raise generic funds for SDG purposes, rather than a single theme such as green or social. In developing countries however, the relative advantage of a social, sustainability, or green bond has been often discussed in the context of the added costs of issuing and monitoring sustainability indicators, versus the additional financial incentives to an issuer in the form of lower capital costs. Faced with similar pricing on a sustainability bond and a vanilla bond, Asian issuers often question the commercial imperative of sustainability bonds and the necessity of undertaking the added diligence required for such bonds. While the increase in funds available from global pools of capital for sustainability-linked bonds is certainly a favorable trend, the fact remains that many infrastructure projects are simply "unbankable" and require concessional finance, or at least structured finance with non- financing incentives to meet sustainability targets. In such a context, pure commercially driven bonds may not find much appeal and indeed may account for the huge gap between needs, estimated by ADB at $1.7 trillion per annum for climate resilient infrastructure in developing Asia, and global SDG bond issuances of only $65 billion in 2019.[23]

E. SDG Accelerator Bond

Though there are many instruments, it is useful to differentiate SDG bonds from other sustainability instruments. The value of the SDG framework lies in its interdisciplinary links, bringing multiple aspects of development together and encouraging synergies. In the time of COVID-19, the focus on inclusion embedded in the SDG framework takes on great relevance and finding a way to increase inclusion while mobilizing financing for recovery is particularly important.

As a potential additional financing mechanism to complement ongoing efforts to address the challenges and increase sustainable finance, this publication suggests structured SDG bonds that can link an acceptable return over a period, to project performance. An SDG accelerator bond (SAB), with three possible structures (conventional payments, deferred payments, or a zero-coupon bond) will aim to provide returns to investors in line with comparable sustainability instruments over the tenor, with an option to exit at predefined project completion or operational dates. The SAB could be designed to enable cheaper funds for projects as an incentive to achieve SDG targets faster.

---

[23]   ADB. 2017. *Meeting Asia's Infrastructure Needs*. Manila.

With schools closed, children are homeschooled.
(photos by Aaron/ADB)

2 Types of Thematic Bonds

The bond market has seen significant growth in thematic instruments creating a plethora of terms and labels, such as socially responsible investing (SRI); environmental, social, and governance (ESG); responsible, etc. With the prominence over the last decade of the 2015 Paris Agreement and the 2012 SDGs, there has been an increase in green bonds, sustainability bonds, social bonds, and transition bonds. There are more than 30 different names for bonds and other debt issuances containing an environmental, social, or governance component. Some thematic bond issuances address environmental concerns, such as green bonds, blue or water bonds, and forest bonds. Others are named after the sector for which the financing is being raised, such as education, housing, gender, etc. Still others are known as sustainability or SDG-linked bonds to signal a commitment by the issuer to specific themes. Figure 9 outlines the relationship among these themes and shows that clearly there is much overlap among the various types of bonds. For instance, the Climate Bonds Initiative (CBI) offers examples of debt labels to describe the types of projects, activities, or expenditures financed, and/or their benefits in the sustainable debt market, under the three main themes: "Green," "Social," and "Sustainability," as shown in Figure 10.[24]

Defining the underlying economic rationale of each type of bond is particularly relevant in the context of public offerings on the international markets, which require detailed disclosure with respect to the types of product offered. A recent survey conducted by the publication Responsible Investor found the use of the term "environmental, social, governance" the least popular among respondents during sustainable finance discussions.[25]

---

[24]   CBI. 2021. *Sustainable Debt: Global State of the Market 2020*. April.
[25]   S. Robinson-Tillett. 2020. Survey: What Words and Phrases Would You Banish from Sustainable Finance Discussions? *Responsible Investor*. 1 June.

Figure 9: Relationships with Green Finance and Other Related Finances

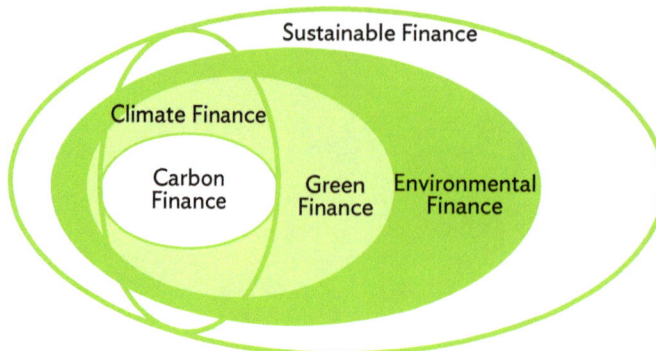

Sustainable Finance

Climate Finance

Carbon Finance

Green Finance

Environmental Finance

Source: H. J. Noh. 2018. Financial Strategy to Accelerate Green Growth. *ADBI Working Paper Series*. No. 866. Tokyo: Asian Development Bank Institute.

Figure 10: Climate Bonds Initiative Debt Labels Under Green, Sustainability and Social Themes

Green	Sustainability	Social
Blue	ESG	Affordable Housing
Climate	Green Innovation	Education, Youth and Employment
Climate Awareness	Positive Impact	Gender Equality
Climate Resilience	SDG	Healthcare
Environmental	Sustainability	SDG Housing
Green	Sustainability Awareness	Social
Renewable Energy	Sustainable Development	Social Housing
Solar	Sustainable Housing	Social Inclusion
Sustainability Awareness		Socially Responsible Investment
Water		Sustainable Development
Wind		University
		Wellbeing
		Women
		Women's Livelihood
		Pandemic
		COVID-19 Social
		COVID-19 Response
		COVID-19 Social Inclusion
		Fight COVID-19
		Vaccine

COVID-19 = coronavirus disease, ESG = environmental, social, and governance, SDG = Sustainable Development Goal.
Source: Climate Bonds Initiative. 2021. *Sustainable Debt: Global State of the Market 2020*. April.

In this line, Pacific Investment Management Company, LLC (PIMCO), one of the biggest bond managers in the world, views SDG bonds as a positive emerging trend and welcomes the two main instruments and structures currently in the market. These are the use of proceeds approach and the linking of the covenant of the bond to the issuer's commitment to reducing climate change or facilitating one or more of the SDGs. PIMCO believes this is a positive step toward the development of the bond market.[26] However, its focus is on how the climate and sustainable strategies of issuers are aligned with their wider corporate strategy and how this lines up with PIMCO's ESG strategy as an investor.

In the context of European high yield, which is typically issued to investors across the globe, including in the United States (US), with reliance on Rule 144A and which requires more detailed disclosure, defining ESG may prove to be an additional challenge. In particular, as the disclosure standard for a 144A transaction requires more detailed information to be provided to investors, care will need to be taken in describing the nature of ESG elements included in the transactions, and in the case of issuances designed to fund specific projects, monitoring the use of proceeds to ensure that they are used for the purpose described in the offering memorandum. In instances where, for example, specific performance metrics are targeted, issuers will need to ensure that the information, including third party reports, provided in an offering memorandum or reporting on an ongoing basis is accurate and verifiable.[27]

Also, courts have shown a willingness to hold fund managers accountable for their representations, including on ESG and corporate social responsibility (CSR) standards (Box 1).

> *"External ESG disclosure standards from regulators, particularly the European Commission, may drive issuers to consider their ESG credentials even more carefully. The European Commission's Action Plan on Sustainable Finance aims to create a Taxonomy Regulation to reduce confusion in identifying green financial products and a Disclosure Regulation requiring asset managers to identify a sustainable investment target and formulate policies on integrating sustainability risks into their investment decisions. The Disclosure Regulation was agreed in March 2019 and is currently moving through the EU legislative process. Potential issuers should start thinking about how these regulatory constraints on investors will affect the market for their high yield bonds"*
>
> **Clifford Chance**

A clear understanding of the express or implied risks associated with representations made regarding the scope of each ESG-themed financial product is thus critical.

Box 1: Failure to Comply with Internal Representations

In a widely cited, early 2008 Pax World Management Corp. case, the US Securities and Exchange Commission (SEC) found that a fund's failures to comply with its own self-imposed socially responsible investing (SRI) policies did violate US securities law—even where the actions had caused no loss to the investors: "Pax World failed to adhere to the SRI restrictions set forth in the prospectuses, SAIs [statements of additional information] and other published material Pax World prepared and filed on behalf of the Funds, and it failed to comply with its own internal SRI screening and periodic review policies which had been disclosed to the Fund boards." (para. 26)

"Pax World misrepresented that it adhered to the SRI restrictions set forth in the prospectuses, SAIs and other published material Pax World prepared and filed on behalf of the Funds." (par. 28)(SEC Release 2008-157).

Source: C. Shrof and D. Constantin. 2015. Corporate Social Responsibility: An Asian Perspective. *Conventus Law*. 13 August.

---

[26] S. Mary, C. Schuetz, and O. A. Albrecht. 2019. SDG Bonds: Their Time Has Come. *PIMCO*. 28 October.
[27] C. Chance. 2019. *From Junk Bonds to Just Bonds: The Increasing Importance of ESG Financing In European High Yield*. Clifford Chance. London.

Some of the more common bond categories that have emerged are:

(i) **ESG bonds.** ESG bonds may generally refer to any issue with an ESG aspect (including green bonds or social bonds). The term is increasingly used though to specifically refer to products linked to an issuer's overall sustainability credentials (as opposed to use-of-proceeds bonds). Under the latter definition, an issuer's performance is measured by their sustainability and ethical impact, with bonds benchmarked against environmental, social, and governance factors. There are no restrictions on how proceeds from these bonds can be used, which helps explain their growing popularity.

(ii) **Green bonds.** Defined by the International Capital Market Association (ICMA) as bonds that enable capital-raising and investment for new and existing projects with environmental benefits. Green bond taxonomies can indicate the sectors eligible for financing from bond proceeds and include renewable energy, energy efficiency, pollution prevention and control, urban and mass transit, circular economy adapted products, green buildings, and marine protection.

(iii) **Social bonds.** Like green bonds, social bonds are use-of-proceeds products and the funds raised must be used for defined social outcomes. Social project categories include affordable basic infrastructure, access to essential services, affordable housing, employment generation, food security, and socioeconomic advancement. The first social bonds were issued to fund the child vaccination provided by Global Alliance for Vaccines and Immunization (GAVI), and the GAVI's International Finance Facility for Immunization (IFFI), offered in 2007, 8 months before the first green bond issuance by the European Investment Bank (EIB). This type of bonds could "eclipse" the green bond market, according to some bankers.[28]

(iv) **Social development bonds and development impact bonds.** Similar to social bonds, these types are used for non-environmental projects that benefit society, such as education, affordable housing, or food security. Unlike social bonds, they do not provide fixed cash flows, and have been said to be similar to equity type products. In effect, they create a contract between private investors and donors or governments who have agreed upon a shared development goal. The investors pay in advance for interventions to reach the goals and are remunerated if the interventions succeed, according to the Center for Global Development.[29] Returns on the bonds are linked to a verified progress outcome.

(v) **Sustainability bonds.** These are bond instruments where the proceeds will be exclusively applied to finance or refinance a combination of green and social projects. Sustainability bonds are usually aligned with the ICMA's Sustainable Bond Guidelines or the Sustainability Bond Principles. Sustainability-linked bonds are a variant where the financing or structuring of the bond's coupon rate is linked to the entity's achievement of set key performance indicators and environmental and/or ESG objectives, failing which there is an uptick of the coupon rate as a penalty. These are also aligned to the ICMA's Sustainability Bond principles.

(vi) **Transition bonds.** They are a relatively new class of bonds that aim to help companies in industries with high greenhouse gas (GHG) emissions (known as brown industries) raise capital specifically to finance decarbonization. Given the urgency of meeting the Paris Agreement's temperature targets, it is seen as imperative that dirty industries transition rapidly from brown to green to make mitigation targets feasible.

---

28 H. Avery. 2016. CSR Bonds: Are Sustainability Bonds Better than Green? *Euromoney*. 23 September.

29 Center for Global Development, Development Impact Bond Working Group. 2013. *Investing in Social Outcomes: Development Impact Bonds*. 7 October.

(vii) **SDG bonds.** They are defined by referencing one or more of the 17 SDGs under the 2030 Agenda for Sustainable Development agreed by all UN Member States. Target projects must make a demonstrable contribution to at least one of the SDGs. According to one issuer, the UN Conference on Trade and Development estimates that globally achieving the SDGs will require $5 trillion to $7 trillion in investment each year from 2015 to 2030. While government spending and development assistance will contribute, they are not expected to total more than $1 trillion per year. The SDGs offer investors the opportunity to use a different lens through which to analyze investment decisions. If investors believe that providing solutions to sustainability challenges offers attractive investment opportunities, they can implement investment strategies that explicitly target SDG themes and sectors[30]

> *"Every large company has a sustainability department and a focus on Corporate Social Responsibility, and social bonds or sustainability bonds allow companies more freedom around the range of initiatives to support via a bond"*
>
> **Navindu Katugampola, head of Sustainable Investing for Morgan Stanley Investment Management Fixed Income & Liquidity**
>
> *"Social bonds will allow fixed income institutional investors the opportunity to become more comfortable with the concept of investments where the proceeds are used for social good"*
>
> *"Social bonds and green bonds go through a strict approval process that investors understand. That could open them up to conversations about other potential investments like pay of success financing"*
>
> **Suzanne Buchta, managing director, Green Bonds, Bank of America Merrill Lynch**

Numerous instruments have been used by various organizations, and it is useful to differentiate the SDG bonds. All countries that have signed up to the SDGs are at different stages of planning and implementation to achieve the targets. Following the Addis Ababa Action Agenda in 2015, the Financing for Development forum, a global framework for financing sustainable development, aligns financial flows with socioeconomic and environmental factors. Its core areas of international finance and development cooperation and elements of debt sustainability will be key in the post-COVID-19 financing era. [31] Similarly, the UN High-Level Political Forum tracks the SDGs and the 2030 Sustainable Development agenda as part of the Economic and Social Council which will report to the United Nations General Assembly later in 2020.[32]

Most countries are guided by these global development frameworks (with globally agreed monitoring and evaluation), though there are limitations in linking the SDGs to project outcomes. Private sector actors are taking these on board and embedding them in their actions through the use of various instruments.

The SDG framework, however, should not be perceived as retrofitting any ESG instrument that has development benefit. The value of the SDG framework lies in its interdisciplinary nature, bringing multiple aspects of development together and encouraging synergies. In the time of COVID-19, the focus on inclusion embedded in the SDG framework takes on great relevance and trying to increase inclusion while mobilizing financing for recovery is particularly important.

Green, social, sustainability, and SDG bonds are no different from normal bonds as far as the transaction process goes (i.e., appointing a banker, arranger, rating agency, etc.). However, some key strategic and process issues distinguish them from conventional bonds. This needs to be considered during the issuing process.

---

[30] D. Wigan. 2019. Caixa Opens Spanish Market for SDG Bonds. *The Banker*. 1 November.
[31] United Nations Sustainable Development Goals. Financing for Sustainable Development.
[32] United Nations Sustainable Development Goals. High-Level Political Forum on Sustainable Development.

Figure 11 summarizes the steps to issuing a green bond. A similar process will also be followed for other thematic bonds issuances.

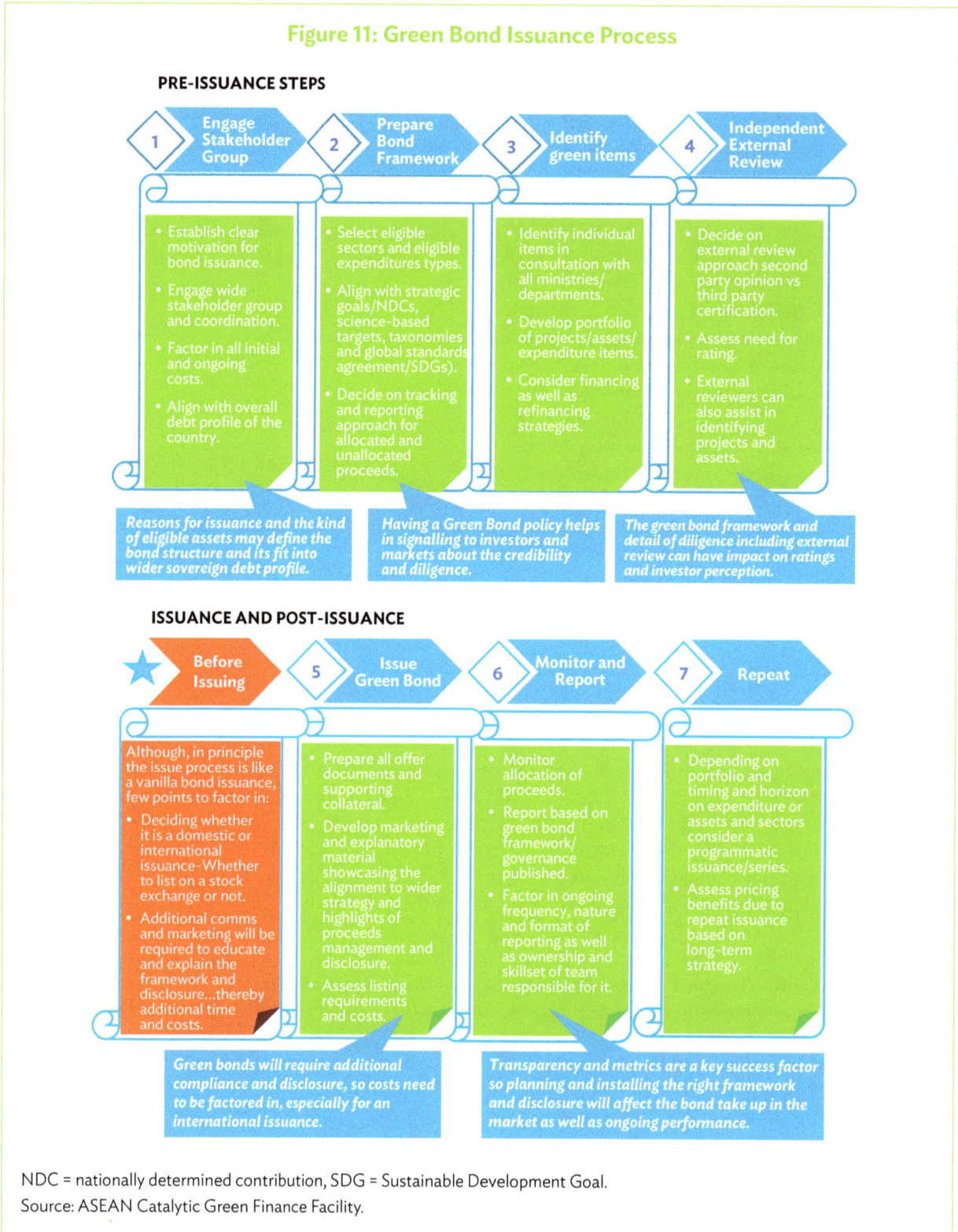

Figure 11: Green Bond Issuance Process

PRE-ISSUANCE STEPS

1 Engage Stakeholder Group
- Establish clear motivation for bond issuance.
- Engage wide stakeholder group and coordination.
- Factor in all initial and ongoing costs.
- Align with overall debt profile of the country.

2 Prepare Bond Framework
- Select eligible sectors and eligible expenditures types.
- Align with strategic goals/NDCs, science-based targets, taxonomies and global standards agreement/SDGs).
- Decide on tracking and reporting approach for allocated and unallocated proceeds.

3 Identify green items
- Identify individual items in consultation with all ministries/departments.
- Develop portfolio of projects/assets/expenditure items.
- Consider financing as well as refinancing strategies.

4 Independent External Review
- Decide on external review approach second party opinion vs third party certification.
- Assess need for rating.
- External reviewers can also assist in identifying projects and assets.

Reasons for issuance and the kind of eligible assets may define the bond structure and its fit into wider sovereign debt profile.

Having a Green Bond policy helps in signalling to investors and markets about the credibility and diligence.

The green bond framework and detail of diligence including external review can have impact on ratings and investor perception.

ISSUANCE AND POST-ISSUANCE

★ Before Issuing
Although, in principle the issue process is like a vanilla bond issuance, few points to factor in:
- Deciding whether it is a domestic or international issuance-Whether to list on a stock exchange or not.
- Additional comms and marketing will be required to educate and explain the framework and disclosure...thereby additional time and costs.

5 Issue Green Bond
- Prepare all offer documents and supporting collateral.
- Develop marketing and explanatory material showcasing the alignment to wider strategy and highlights of proceeds management and disclosure.
- Assess listing requirements and costs.

6 Monitor and Report
- Monitor allocation of proceeds.
- Report based on green bond framework/governance published.
- Factor in ongoing frequency, nature and format of reporting as well as ownership and skillset of team responsible for it.

7 Repeat
- Depending on portfolio and timing and horizon on expenditure or assets and sectors consider a programmatic issuance/series.
- Assess pricing benefits due to repeat issuance based on long-term strategy.

Green bonds will require additional compliance and disclosure, so costs need to be factored in, especially for an international issuance.

Transparency and metrics are a key success factor so planning and installing the right framework and disclosure will affect the bond take up in the market as well as ongoing performance.

NDC = nationally determined contribution, SDG = Sustainable Development Goal.
Source: ASEAN Catalytic Green Finance Facility.

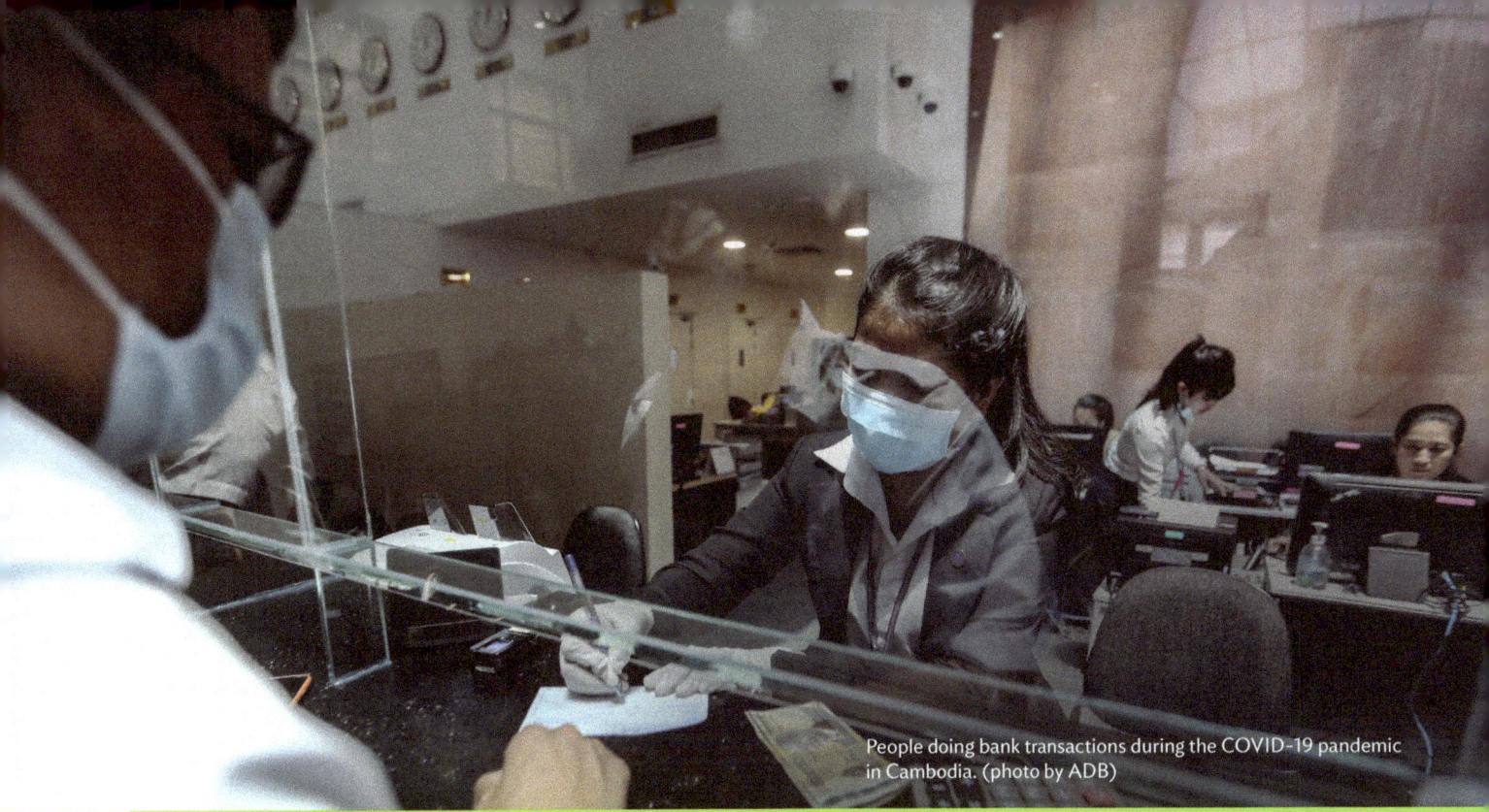

People doing bank transactions during the COVID-19 pandemic in Cambodia. (photo by ADB)

3 SDG Bonds

This chapter presents the evolution and context of SDG bonds issuances in recent years. In this regard, sustainability bonds, sustainability-linked bonds, and green bonds showed a marked growth in 2019 and became an integral part of the overall thematic bonds market. This market was originally dominated by green bonds, often seen as a proxy for the wider market. Figure 12 outlines the market's rapid growth, especially the increase in the share of sustainable and social bonds.

Figure 12: Growth of the Green Finance Market

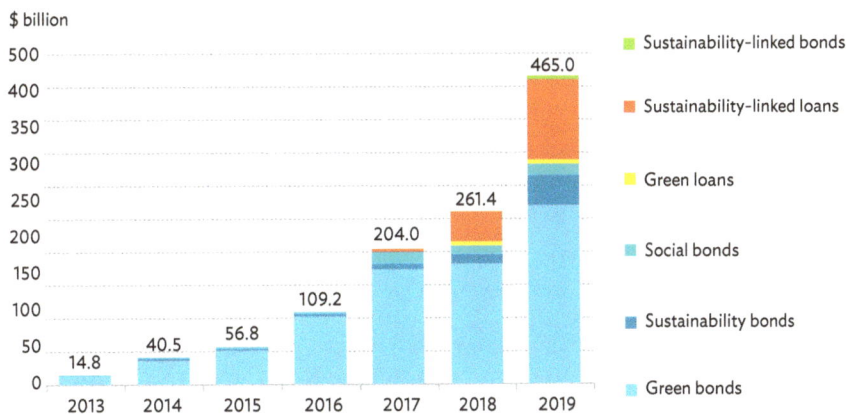

Source: Climate Bonds Initiative. 2020. Climate Bonds Initiative Market Summary H1 2020. August.

More recently, the COVID-19 pandemic has led to a focus on the disparity in social provision in many developing countries, given the severe impact on health, businesses, jobs, and livelihoods. With the need for immediate relief and recovery, the green bond market has been overshadowed by social and sustainable bonds, reflecting the need to shift toward financing for socioeconomic recovery, over and above environmental financing. In addition, the world has renewed its focus on the SDGs, with only 10 years left to achieve them. This may be a causal factor in the recent rise in sustainability bonds and sustainability-linked loans.

Sustainability bond issuances totalled $194.5 billion during the first half of 2020, up 47% from the same period in 2019 and more than double the value recorded during the first 6 months of 2018. In the first half of 2020 alone, issuances in sustainability bonds hit $56.7 billion, which was double the levels seen during the first half of 2019 and accounted for an increase of 94% over the previous year. A total of $130.9 billion worth of sustainable bonds were issued globally during the second quarter of 2020, over double the value of the previous quarter. According to Refinitiv, this was the highest quarterly total since their records began in 2015 (Figure 13).[33]

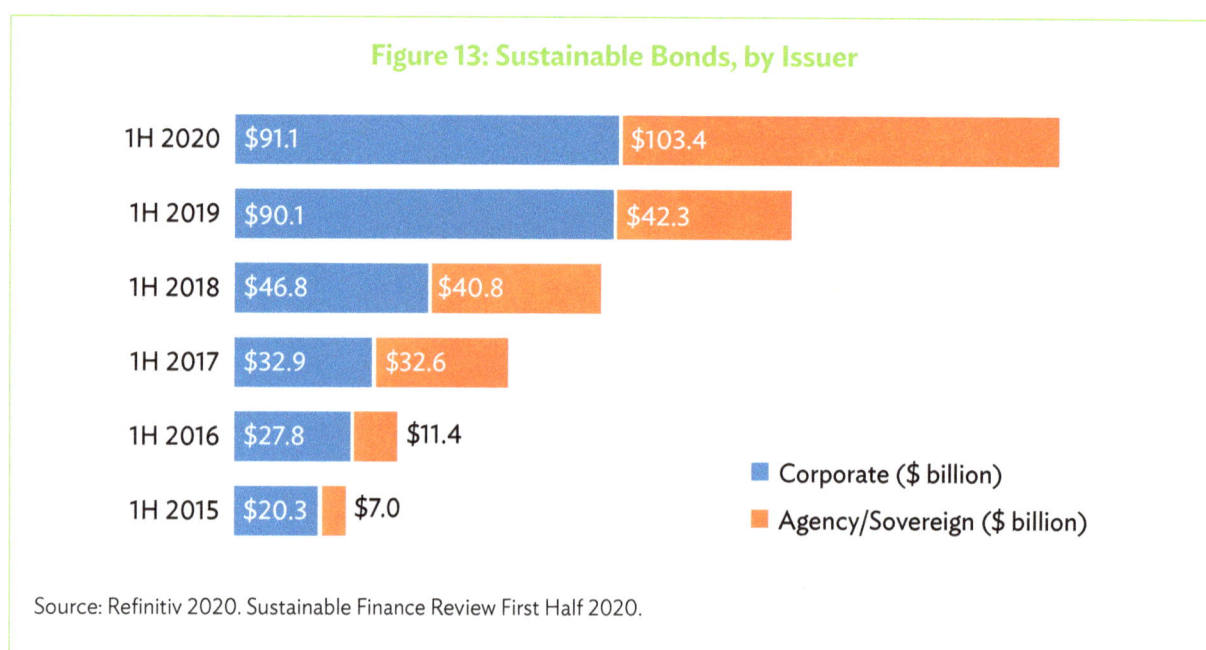

Figure 13: Sustainable Bonds, by Issuer

	Corporate ($ billion)	Agency/Sovereign ($ billion)
1H 2020	$91.1	$103.4
1H 2019	$90.1	$42.3
1H 2018	$46.8	$40.8
1H 2017	$32.9	$32.6
1H 2016	$27.8	$11.4
1H 2015	$20.3	$7.0

Source: Refinitiv 2020. Sustainable Finance Review First Half 2020.

According to Moody's, global sustainable bond issuance topped $99.9 billion in the second quarter of 2020, a quarterly record, and 65% higher than the first quarter. Record quarterly issuance of both social bonds at $33 billion and sustainability bonds at $19.1 billion account for the strong total.[34]

The global bond issuances for initiatives that cater to social sector (such as social bonds by the Republic of Korea and the African Development Bank), unemployment insurance management (by Unidec Asseo), and provision of online services and education (by Peason Plc) have reached $41.9 billion in the first half of 2020, a 376% increase over the same period last year (Figure 14).[35]

---

[33]   Refinitiv 2020. *Sustainable Finance Review First Half 2020.*
[34]   BFSI.com. 2020. Sustainable Bond Issuance Hits Record High in Q2 as Social Bonds Surge: *Moody's.* 17 August.
[35]   D. C. Mutua. 2020. Social Debt Surges to Record as Borrowers Tackle Coronavirus. *Bloomberg.* 30 July.

Figure 14: Social Bonds Total Issuance, 2015–2020
($ billion)

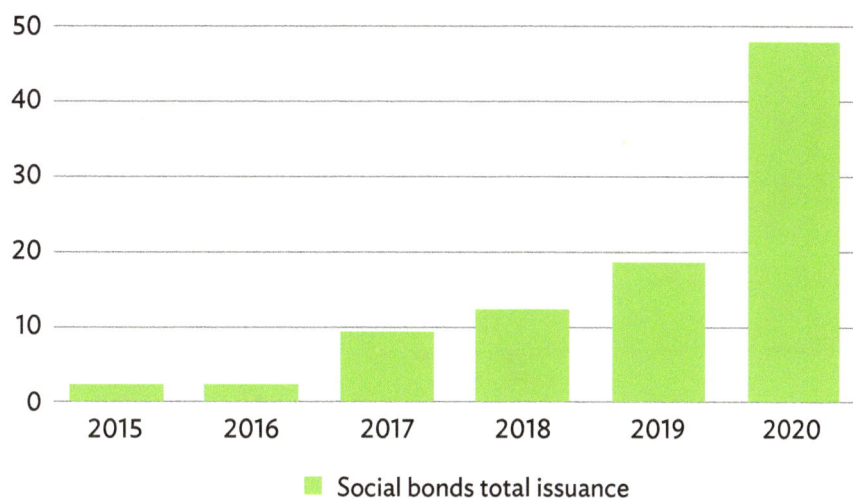

Note: Data for 2015–2019 are full year; for 2020, they are from January to 22 July.

Source: D. C. Mutua. 2020. Social Debt Surges to Record as Borrowers Tackle Coronavirus. *Bloomberg*. 30 July.

A. Selected Precedents

SDG bonds have been issued by four types of institutions: subsovereigns; multilateral and bilateral agencies; private sector financial institutions; and private corporations. Table 1 provides a summary of the various types of issuances (ICMA n.d.). A non-limitative list (together with a description) of these types of issuances is presented in Appendix 1.

Table 1: Examples of SDG Bonds

Issuer	Size	Date	Tenor (year)	Coupon and Price	Listing
SUBSOVEREIGNS					
Madrid Regional Government (Spain)	€1.25 billion	April 2019	10.0	1.57%	
NRW State (Germany)	€1 billion	November 2019	10.0	0	
	€1.5 billion	November 2018	20.0	0.5%	
Region Ile-de-France (France)	€500 million	June 2018	15.0	1.375%	
Flemish government (Belgium)	€750 million	June 2019	25.0	1.567%	
	€500 million	November 2018	15.0	1.375%	

continued on next page

Table 1 *continued*

Issuer	Size	Date	Tenor (year)	Coupon and Price	Listing
MULTILATERALS					
World Bank	Can$1.5 billion	26 July 2019 (settlement date)	5.0	CAN 1½ 09 January 2024 + 35bps 1.8 %	Luxembourg
	€1.5 billion	21 May 2019 (settlement date)	10.0	Bund +36.8 bps 0.25 %	Luxembourg Dublin
IDB	Mex$395 million	27 November 2019 (settlement date)	3.5	5.64 %	
	Mex$444 million	27 November 2019 (settlement date)	7.0	0 %	
	£275 million	22 October 2019 (settlement date)	7.0	UKT 1.5% 22 July 2026 +43 bps 0.5 %	London
	Can$600 million	10 October 2019 (settlement date)	5.0	UKT 1.5% 10 October 2024 +43 bps 1.7 %	London
FINANCIAL INSTITUTIONS					
Kasikornbank (Thailand)	$100 million	October 2018	5.0	This was the first sustainability bond from a Thai issuer and the first such bond from ASEAN financial institutions. These senior, unsecured bonds had a floating interest rate based on LIBOR plus 0.95 percentage points.	
RCBC (Philippines)	₱8 billion	June 2019	2.0	Issued as ASEAN Sustainability Bonds, the first of its kind in the Philippines under the ASEAN Sustainability Bond Standards 2018. Coupon of 6.15% per annum to be paid quarterly until May 2021.	
RCBC (Philippines)	$300 million	September 2019	5.0	Sustainability notes were issued at 99.751 with a coupon rate of 3% per annum. These are offshore notes to be listed on the Singapore Exchange Securities Trading Ltd. five times oversubscribed from base.	
BPI (Philippines)	₱2.1 billion	August 2020	1.8	BPI issued its first peso-denominated social bond. These are COVID Action Response or "CARE" bonds focusing on COVID-19 response efforts, were seven times oversubscribed and were part of a ₱100-billion bond program. The CARE bonds were aligned to ASEAN social bond standards and the proceeds were used to help small businesses.	

continued on next page

Table 1 *continued*

Issuer	Size		Date	Tenor (year)	Coupon and Price		Listing
Development Bank of (Philippines)	P18.125 billion		November 2019	2	4.25%		PDex
PT Bank Rakyat ("BRI") (Indonesia)	$500 million		March 2019	5.0	This is the first sustainability bond from one of Indonesia's largest banks and is financing green and social bond projects in Indonesia. Coupon of 3.95% is paid semi-annually. This bond is oversubscribed more than eight times.		
Grupo Bancolombia (Colombia)	COL$657 million		June 2019 (approved)	5.0	Private placement. Structured, and 100% subscribed, by IDB Invest, a member of IDB group		
Banistmo (Panama)	$50 million		March 2019 (approved)	5.0			
CaixaBank (Spain)	€1 billion		September 2019 (announced)	5.0	mid-swap + 113 bps 0.625%		
ANZ (New Zealand)	€1 billion		November 2019 (announced)	10.0	mid-swap + 140 bps		
	€750 million		February 2018 (announced)	5.0	swap + 15 bps 0.643%		ASX
CORPORATES							
Starbucks (US)	$1 billion		May 2019 (announced)	30.0	4.450%		
	¥85 billion		March 2017 (announced)	7.0	0.372%		
	$500 million		May 2016 (announced)	10.0	2.450%		
Enel (Italy)	€2.5 billion	T1: €1 billion	October 2019 (announced)	5.0	0%		Ireland
		T2: €1 billion		8.0	0.375%		
		T3: €500 million		15.0	1.125%		
	$1.5 billion		September 2019	5.0			
Manila Water Co Inc (Philippines)	€500 million Sustainability Notes		July 2020	5	4.5%		PDex

€ = euro, ₱ = Philippine peso, £ = pound sterling, ¥ = Japanese yen, ANZ = Australia and New Zealand Banking Group, ASEAN = Association of Southeast Asian Nations, ASX = Australian Securities Exchange, BPI = Bank of the Philippine Islands, bps = basis points, CAN = Canada, Can$ = Canadian dollar, COVID-19 = coronavirus disease, IDB = Inter-American Development Bank, LIBOR = London interbank offered rate, Mex$ = Mexican peso, NRW = North Rhine-Westphalia, RCBC = Rizal Commercial Banking Corporation, SDG = Sustainable Development Goal, UKT = United Kingdom Treasury, US = United States.

Source: Asian Development Bank.

Initiatives by the public sector to participate in this arena to raise capital have been relatively few to date, primarily in Europe.

The sovereign green bond issuance in 2019 was strong through the year, which in the first half (H1) of 2019 accounted for 15% of total green bond issuance (increase over 12% recorded over similar period in 2018). Many sovereigns debuted in 2019 including the Dutch State Treasury and Hong Kong, China. New sovereign bonds were issued by Chile, Poland, Indonesia and Nigeria, while France, Belgium, and the Irish National Treasury Management Agency tapped their original issuances. The issuances from local governments and government backed entities aggregated $24.8 billion in H1 (more than double the $9.6 billion issued in H1 2018). A total of 64 issuers from 16 countries contributed to this volume, 15% of which was issued by new entrants. France contributed to 13% of H1 issuance. The US and Sweden municipalities had similar share of issuances. German KfW (who expanded its use of proceeds to include low-carbon buildings) was the largest issuer with $4.1 billion. For the full year 2019, government backed-entities accounted for approximately 15% of all green bond issuances. Kommuninvest, Landesbank Baden-Wurttemberg (LBBW), Orsted, Societe nationale des chemins de fer francais (SNCF) and Societe du Grand Paris are the top five issuers with an aggregate of $14.2 billion.[36]

At the end of 2019, total sustainability and SDG bond issuances accounted for $65 billion, tripling from $21 billion in 2018. German development bank Land NRW ($2.6 billion), American café chain Starbucks ($1 billion, repeat issuer) and Belgian local government Flemish Community ($845 million, debut issuer) were some of the largest issuers in the sustainability segment in 2019.[37]

Looking into Southeast Asia, Thailand issued its first sustainability bond of B30 billion (about $964 million), in August 2020, and accessed the market again in November 2020 with a further tap of B20 billion (about $667 million) to refinance the MRT asset pool, bringing the total bond outstanding to date to B50 billion (about $1.65 billion). Thailand's National Housing Authority (NHA) announced the issuance of a social bond investing in affordable housing. ADB has been working closely with both Thailand's Public Debt Management Office (PDMO) and NHA as part of wider green and COVID-19 recovery support in the region that will help Thailand tackle climate change in line with the Paris Agreement and the SDGs (Box 2).[38] These national objectives are part of the Sufficient Economy Philosophy and the government's 20-year National Strategy Framework, reinforced by its 12th National Economic and Social Development Plan (2016–2020). ADB's continuing technical assistance to sustainability and social bond issuance encompasses external reviews for aligning with global standards and best practices. These are laid out by ICMA, the ASEAN Capital Markets Forum (ACMF), and the Loan Market Association (LMA). ADB also supports the development of internal systems to monitor use of proceeds and prepare post-issuance reports. This will also help facilitate subsequent sovereign issuances of thematic bonds (green, social, and sustainability) over the coming years.

Table 2: Thailand's Bonds for a Social, Sustainable, and Green COVID-19 Recovery

Issuer	Size	Issue Date	Tenor	Coupon
Kingdom of Thailand (Public Debt Management Office)	B30 billion B20 billion	August 2020 November 2020	15 years	1.585% 1.65%
National Housing Authority	B6.8 billion across 3 tranches B1 billion B2.8 billion B3 billion	September 2020	 5 years 10 years 15 years	 1.02% 1.64% 1.90%

B = Thai baht, COVID-19 = coronavirus disease.
Source: ASEAN Catalytic Green Finance Facility.

---

[36] CBI. 2019. *Green bonds market H1 2019*. July.
[37] CBI. 2020. *2019 Green Bond Market Summary*. February.
[38] ADB. 2020. *ADB Supports Thailand's Green, Social, and Sustainability Bonds for COVID-19 Recovery*. 24 September.

Box 2: ADB Supports Thailand's Bond Program for a Sustainable and Green COVID-19 Recovery

Thailand, acting through its Ministry of Finance, issued a benchmark bond series under its Sustainable Financing Framework, accessing the capital markets for a post-coronavirus disease (COVID-19) green recovery in August 2020.

Thailand's sustainability bond, issued through the Public Debt Management Office (PDMO) in August 2020, offers two tranches of fixed rate government bonds for a total principal aggregate amount of B30 billion (about $964 million). The Government of Thailand accessed the market again in November 2020 with a further tap of B20 billion ($667 million) to refinance the MRT asset pool, bringing the total bond outstanding to date to B50 billion ($1.65 billion). It is one of the first such sovereign bonds globally that combines green as well as social impacts with COVID-19 recovery. The bond was oversubscribed three times and its proceeds will be used to finance green infrastructure in Bangkok's Mass Rapid Transit Orange Line (East) Project which was certified against Climate Bonds Standards under its low carbon transport sector criteria, as well as other social projects supporting the country's COVID-19 recovery and Sustainable Development Goals (SDGs) 3 and 8, including public health care and employment generation. These will form part of a wider 15-year benchmark bond program of an amount no less than B100,000 million over the next 2 fiscal years (2020–2021 and 2021–2022; a fiscal year in Thailand goes from 1 October to 30 September of the next year) covering wider green sectors as well as targeted support for economic recovery in the post-COVID-19 period.

The National Housing Authority of Thailand also issued a social bond in September 2020 in three tranches totalling B6.8 billion (about $223 million). The bond was oversubscribed by B1.4 billion (about $46 million) and its proceeds will fund affordable housing (SDG 11) and refinance their portfolio of residential real estate for low- and middle-income earners with a view to providing cohesive communities and better living conditions. It is among the first social bonds issued by a state-owned enterprise in Southeast Asia. The social bond framework and the program will contribute to reducing inequality and poverty and looks to incorporate green building and energy efficiency as part of commitments to SDGs 1, 3, 5, 7, and 10.

ADB = Asian Development Bank.
Source: ADB. Government of Thailand. 2020. *Sustainability Bond Issuance: Investor Presentation*. July.

B. SDG Bonds Features

The SDG bond issuance features to date vary depending on the stakeholder group.

(i) **Subsovereigns**
   (a) Primarily issued by European subsovereigns, with limited examples in other countries (e.g., Mexico).
   (b) The tenor range is usually longer than that of issuances by corporates (10–25 years).

(ii) **Multilateral and bilateral agencies**
   (a) The capital is raised for potentially on-lending to member countries focused on specific SDGs, though evidence of a strong link between project outcomes and the relevant SDG is still evolving.
   (b) The rating of the instrument is typically AAA.
   (c) The investors are banks (and their treasuries), central banks, official institutions, pension funds, insurance companies, and asset managers. There is not much evidence of participation by retail investors.
   (d) Investors are primarily from Europe and the Americas, with limited participation from Asian investors.
   (e) The tenor of the issuances ranges from 3 to 10 years and the pricing is based on the country or region targeted.
   (f) While many international financial institutions are trying to raise their environmental standards, this varies by region, with Asia being slower than other regions. Typically, environment safeguards apply when multilaterals are offering their assistance.

(iii) **Financial institutions**

(a) The capital is raised by the financial institutions to support projects aimed at achieving specific SDGs.

(b) The ratings are lower than those instruments issued by the multilateral and bilateral agencies, typically in the BBB range.

(c) The investors include multilateral agencies and other banks, as well as institutional agencies.

(d) The region is primarily Europe and the Americas, there are fewer initiatives in Asia and Australia.

(e) The tenor varies from 5 to 10 years and returns are generally in line with the market. Some non-bank financial institutions say they aim to achieve superior financial returns through buying stocks from companies that are in the early stage of implementing pro-SDG practices in their own operations and across their value chains.[39]

(f) While pricing spreads are important to financial institutions, the risk weighting for green and sustainable financing also adds to the cost. A lower risk weighting (in the form of capital relief or waivers on withholding taxes) might enable them to pass the savings on to customers thereby accelerating projects.

(iv) **Corporates**

(a) Corporates have raised capital to meet their ordinary financial requirements, either targeted toward specific SDGs or multi-SDG goals.

(b) The bonds come with different structures (tranches) to suit participating investors.

(c) The regional focus is Europe and the Americas, with financial institutions being the preferred investor group.

(d) There is limited evidence to support the price advantage of SDG Bonds. A recent study by JP Morgan Asset Management has concluded that adding an ESG overlay can improve returns and reduce volatility.[40] Only one corporate (Enel) has indicated that they have obtained a discount in SDG bond issuance in relation to their issuance of comparable non-sustainability bonds. Enel has also linked the coupon rates to achievement of stated SDGs. If the SDGs are not achieved, they will pay a higher coupon to the investor.[41]

(e) The corporate bonds have a second party opinion that confirms the use-of-proceeds.

C. SDG Bonds Funds Usage

Funds raised through sustainability bonds can be used in a broad range of sectors, often in multi-sectoral projects. For instance, proceeds from the Rizal Commercial Banking Corporation (RCBC) June 2019 sustainability bonds were to be used to fund projects in the following sectors: renewable energy, green buildings, clean transportation, energy efficiency, pollution prevention and control, sustainable water management, and other areas.

In the case of the sustainability bond issued by Kasikornbank in Thailand, 65% of the funds were allocated to green projects and 35% to social projects. Green projects included renewable energy (solar energy and waste-to-energy) projects, and green buildings. Social projects focused on employment generation and access to essential services.

---

[39] R. Walker. 2019. Hermes Launches SDG High Yield Bond Funds. *Fund Selector Asia*. 27 September.

[40] JPMorgan Chase & Co. 2019. *Environmental Social and Governance Report 2019.*

[41] *Enel*. 2019. Enel Launches the World's First "General Purpose SDG Linked Bond", Successfully Placing a 1.5 Billion U.S. Dollar Bond on the U.S. Market. 6 September.

D. Alternative Approaches

A number of alternative options have recently been tested in the market by private financial institutions, multilaterals, and development agencies in an attempt to hedge against difficulties with traditional (green, social and sustainability) use-of-proceeds bonds.

Such bonds are premised on the allocation of funds to specific, certified projects and on payment of regular interest to investors at fixed-rate coupons, with or without a discount, reflecting the general attractiveness of these products for institutional buyers. But these bond issuances have been criticized for lack of commitment to environmental, social, and governance standards, as well as for unreliable monitoring.

Coupons on green and other use-of-proceeds bonds are usually fixed and unrelated to the wider ESG performance of the company. One of the main controversies centers around "greenwashing," or overstating the environmental benefits of a project. This is despite oversight by external, independent verifiers with a mandate limited to specific projects. Having an exclusion list is increasingly seen as a complement to ensuring that projects attribute links to the SDGs appropriately. This differs from the outcome-driven structure of SDG-linked bonds, such as the Enel bonds, as well as loans. "We would rather see companies improve their full corporate wide ESG profile than spending too much time identifying a specific project that meets all the qualifications for it to be a green bond," the head of US Stewardship and Sustainable Investments for Legal & General Investment Management America, John Hoeppner, told the International Financing Review in May 2019.[42]

Sustainability-linked loans are growing in popularity with $62 billion raised in the first 9 months of 2019, which is more than the aggregate raised in 2018. Borrowers of these loans, particularly in Europe, often receive ESG-related incentives for revolving credit facilities and term loans, wherein the interest rates are tied to achieving measurable key performance indicators (such as waste or emissions levels, or to an independent ESG rating). There are no other significant restrictions on the use of proceeds for such loans. The uptake in these sustainability linked loans contrast with the decline in the use of green loans, where funds have to be used for specified environmental purposes. Enel adopted a similar structure in its bond version that links the ESG outcomes with its pricing.[43]

Interestingly, some ESG-linked products (and Enel bonds specifically) have also been suspected of "greenwashing" by some investors and activists, due to the way the respective bond was structured. Under the provisions of such products, Enel has the flexibility to use the proceeds in a manner that is best suited to its needs, even for a coal-powered electricity generation project, and is not bound to specify how the money is spent. Enel believes that the organization is geared toward ambitious clean energy goals, and products like these give flexibility to achieve the same. These new formats of SDG-linked bonds, however, have not found the support of some green investors, who believe that these go against the accountability and transparency norms.[44]

There are no universal metric or performance indicators yet for social bonds (unlike for green bonds, which have evolved over the last decade), even if private sector organizations and multilaterals are working toward common standards. Investment professionals have expressed concern about social bonds: "While a recent BNP Paribas roundtable found investors increasingly open to the idea of social bonds as a means of delivering positive impact while generating a satisfactory return, concerns remain. First, liquidity is low; second, impact reporting standards have not been settled. Until these concerns are addressed, issuers and investors may be cautious: the integrity of the market underpinned by robust frameworks is necessary for market development."[45]

---

[42]   *International Finance Review.* 2019. Borrowers Respond to Bondholder Demand on ESG Standards. 23 May.

[43]   J. Poh. 2019. ESG Debt: A User's Guide to Ever-Growing Menu of Bonds And Loans. *Bloomberg.* 16 October.

[44]   G. Gore. 2019. UPDATE 1-Enel Ditches Green Bonds for Controversial New Format. *Reuters.* 4 October.

[45]   A. Gourc. 2019. Social Bonds: The Next Frontier for ESG Investors. BNP Paribas. 23 July.

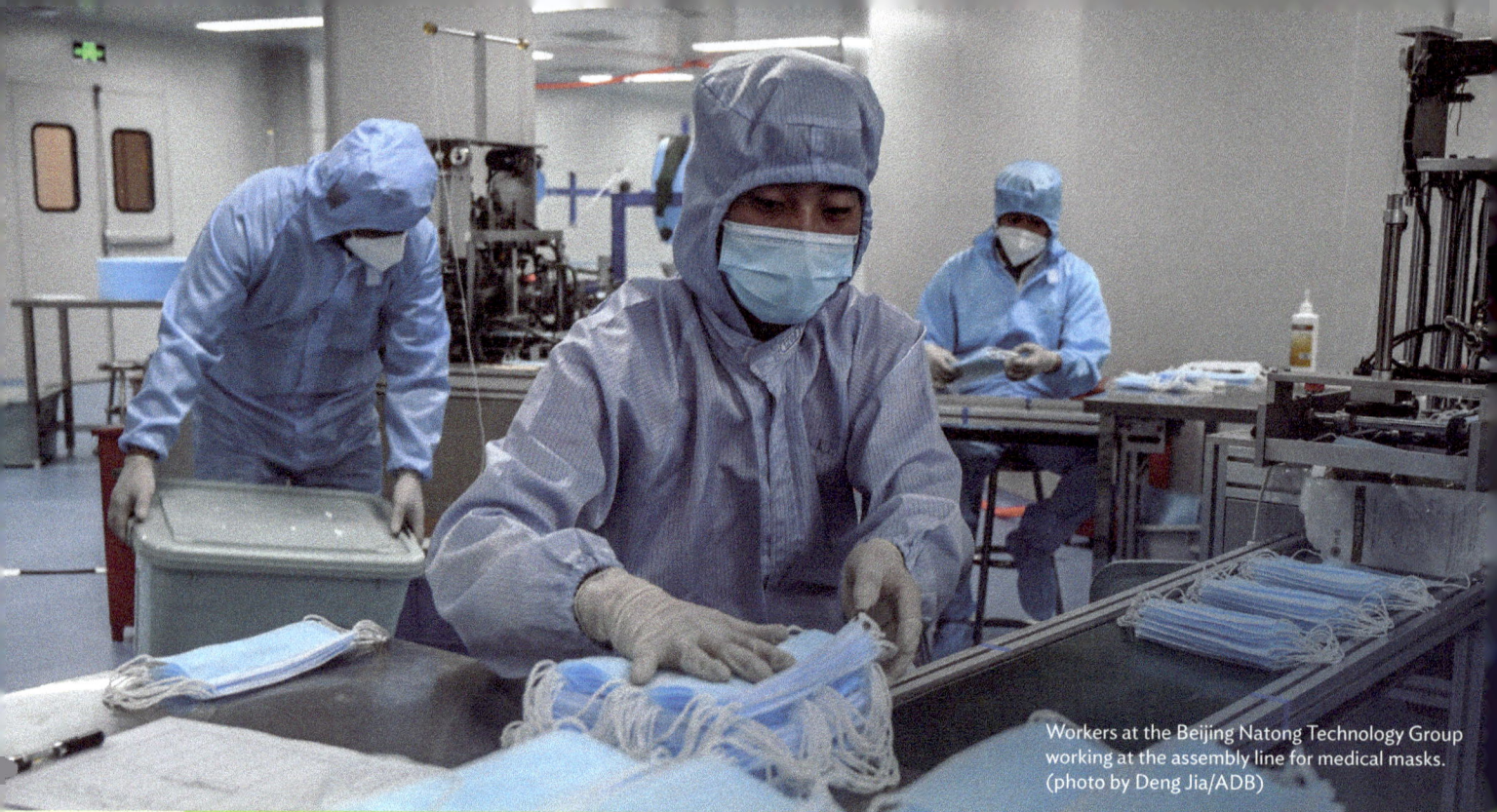

Workers at the Beijing Natong Technology Group working at the assembly line for medical masks. (photo by Deng Jia/ADB)

<table>
<tr><td>4</td><td># Standards, Guidelines, and Frameworks</td></tr>
</table>

4 Standards, Guidelines, and Frameworks

A clear usage-of-funds framework is critical for any bond purporting to raise funds for social impact purposes. For use-of-proceeds bonds, including SDG bonds, it is critical that issuers are able to monitor the project-specific implementation of the commitment by issuers to SDG targets. Issuers must ensure that the proceeds are effectively used for the purposes described in the issuance documents. Deviations or inaccuracies expose issuers to legal action, potential reputational damage, and eventual economic costs.

Over the last decade, stakeholders such as the European Union (EU), the International Capital Markets Association (ICMA), the Climate Bonds Initiative (CBI), and the ASEAN Capital Markets Forum (ACMF), have established standards and guidelines to determine whether or not a bond is eligible for an ESG label. They have also designed frameworks and metrics for the monitoring of the use of bond proceeds. This section elaborates on the details of some of these frameworks as an illustration.

A. The International Capital Markets Association

ICMA membership includes private and public issuers, banks and securities houses, asset managers, capital market infrastructure providers, central banks, law firms, and others. "It makes recommendations and produces guidance notes for issuers and lead managers to follow when doing a bond issue. These recommendations are market standard and should be followed, where possible."[46] The ICMA publishes a number of guidelines:

---

[46]   Thomson Reuters Practical Law. Practical Law. Bond Issues: Step-by-Step Guide.

the Green Bond Principles (GBP), the Social Bond Principles (SBP), and the Sustainability Bond Guidelines (SBG), and the Sustainability-Linked Bond Principles (SLBP). Recently, ICMA published the Climate Transition Finance Handbook that provides guidance on the practices, actions and disclosures to be made available when raising funds for climate transition-related purposes.[47]

In its 2019 report Working Toward a Harmonized Framework for Impact Bond Reporting, the ICMA said: "Overcoming global development challenges and advancing objectives for the public good requires significant investment in projects that bring about positive social impact. Many of these investments are expected to be financed by debt instruments, including bonds. Committing a section of the bond market to the financing of projects with expected positive social outcomes will channel existing and new pools of liquidity to address global challenges such as those exemplified by the SDGs. Due to the nascent stage of the market, the Social Bond Working Group acknowledges that there are a variety of indicators in use and that indicators may measure outputs (the practices, products and services that result from the project), outcomes (the benefits or changes to individuals and/or groups that occur as a result of the outputs), or the long-term impact (the final result of the outcomes and impacts may take several years to become evident after project activities are completed)." In the context of the SDGs, the ICMA's High-level Mapping to the Sustainable Development Goals aims to "provide a broad frame of reference by which issuers, investors and bond market participants can evaluate the financing objectives of a given green, social or sustainability bond or bond programme against the SDGs."[48]

B. The Climate Bonds Initiative

The CBI is an investor focused not-for-profit international organization working solely to mobilize the largest capital market of all, the $100 trillion bond market, for climate change solutions. The Climate Bonds Standard and Certification Scheme act as a labelling scheme for debt instruments using rigorous scientific criteria to ensure that certified instruments are consistent with the 2 degrees Celsius global warming limit in the Paris Agreement. The certification serves as a benchmark of diligence using climate science at a sectoral level. It is used globally by bond issuers, governments, investors and the financial markets to transparently show that the underlying assets genuinely contribute to addressing climate change.

The Climate Bonds Standard provides clear, sector-specific eligibility criteria for assets and projects that can benefit from climate bonds and green bonds (Figure 15).[49] While these standards are largely focused on the environmental and emissions thresholds, because at least six of the SDGs deal with climate or emissions, they see green and climate bonds as a bridge to the SDGs.[50] Further, given the current situation post-COVID-19, and the link between health and the environment as outlined by the World Health Organization (WHO), these standards (which promote diligence) may extend to social and sustainable bonds and loans. Furthermore, climate eligibility criteria can be useful also when assessing other types of social financing. [51]

---

[47]   ICMA. 2020. *Climate Transition Finance Handbook 2020*. December.
[48]   ICMA. 2020. *Green, Social and Sustainability Bonds: A High-Level Mapping to the Sustainable Development Goals*. June.
[49]   CBI. 2019. *Climate Bonds Taxonomy*. October.
[50]   CBI. 2018. Green Bonds: A Bridge to SDGs - Focus on SDG 6, 7, 9, 11, 13 and 15. 20 June.
[51]   WHO. 2018. Climate Change and Health. 1 February.

Figure 15 Climate Bonds Taxonomy

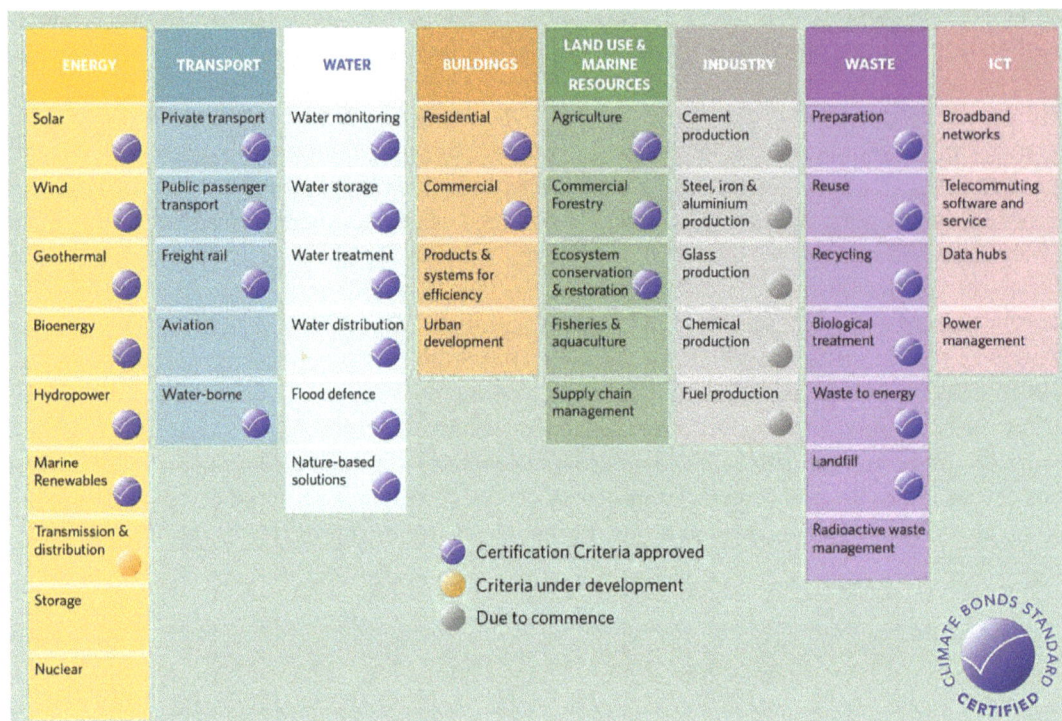

ENERGY	TRANSPORT	WATER	BUILDINGS	LAND USE & MARINE RESOURCES	INDUSTRY	WASTE	ICT
Solar	Private transport	Water monitoring	Residential	Agriculture	Cement production	Preparation	Broadband networks
Wind	Public passenger transport	Water storage	Commercial	Commercial Forestry	Steel, iron & aluminium production	Reuse	Telecommuting software and service
Geothermal	Freight rail	Water treatment	Products & systems for efficiency	Ecosystem conservation & restoration	Glass production	Recycling	Data hubs
Bioenergy	Aviation	Water distribution	Urban development	Fisheries & aquaculture	Chemical production	Biological treatment	Power management
Hydropower	Water-borne	Flood defence		Supply chain management	Fuel production	Waste to energy	
Marine Renewables		Nature-based solutions				Landfill	
Transmission & distribution						Radioactive waste management	
Storage							
Nuclear							

Certification Criteria approved
Criteria under development
Due to commence

CLIMATE BONDS STANDARD CERTIFIED

Source: CBI. 2019. *Climate Bonds Taxonomy*. October.

C. The ASEAN Capital Markets Forum

The ACMF launched the ASEAN Green Bond Standards in 2017, and both the ASEAN Social Bond Standards (ASEAN SBS) and the ASEAN Sustainability Bond Standards (ASEAN SUS) were launched in 2018.[52] "The standards are intended to enhance transparency, consistency and uniformity of ASEAN green, social and sustainability bonds, which will reduce due diligence cost and assist global investors to make informed investment decisions."[53]

The ASEAN Standards have been developed based on ICMA's Principles. The GBP, for example, have been used as the basis of the ASEAN Green Bond, and aim to provide more specific guidance on applying the standards across the region to enable issuers labelling their bonds and demonstrating compliance with the ASEAN Standards.

D. United Nations Standards

Given the different frameworks that are being developed, it is useful to have an official or globally accepted framework for monitoring progress toward the SDGs agreed by all countries. A global indicator framework for the SDGs was developed by the Inter-Agency and Expert Group on SDG Indicators (IAEG-SDGs)

---

[52] ACMF. 2018. ASEAN *Green Bond Standards*. October; ACMF. 2018. *ASEAN Social Bond Standards*. October; ACMF. 2018. *ASEAN Sustainability Bond Standards*. October.

[53] The Asset. 2018. *Asean Launches Social and Sustainability Bond Standards*. 16 October.

and agreed at the 48th session of the United Nations (UN) Statistical Commission in March 2017. It was adopted by the UN General Assembly in July 2017. The global indicator framework includes 231 unique indicators, cross referenced against each SDG. Although the SDG indicator framework remains a work in progress, it could serve as a useful tool for SDG-related investment. For example, UN Economic and Social Commission for Asia and the Pacific (UNESCAP) launched a country guide in 2017 designed to help countries maximize the contribution that their public–private partnership programs and projects make to meeting the SDGs.[54]

A set of practice assurance standards for SDG bonds has also been developed by the United Nations Development Programme (UNDP). These standards are designed to help SDG bond programs define their use-of-proceeds where coupon payment is linked to achieving targets related to specific SDG outcomes. A summary of the standards is shown in Table 3.

Table 3: Summary of Practice Assurance Standards for SDG Bonds

Strategic Intent and Impact Goal Setting	
1	The SDG Bond Program has clearly defined and contextualized SDG impact intentions and strategic impact goals
Impact Measurement and Management	
2	The issuer embeds sound impact measurement and management practices into the design and operation of the SDG Bond Program
3	The issuer establishes Eligibility Criteria to select and undertake ex-ante impact assessments of potential Qualifying Activities for its SDG Bond Program
4	The Issuer systematically measures and manages the ongoing impact performance of its SDG Bond Program
Transparency and Comparability	
5	The issuer discloses information about, and regularly reports on, its SDG Bond Program in a manner that promotes SDG impact integrity, transparency and comparability
Context and Governance	
6	The issuer's governance processes provide the appropriate operating context for, and effective oversight of the SDG Bond Program

SDG = Sustainable Development Goal.
Source: United Nations Development Programme. 2020. *SDG Impact Standards for Bonds*.

Under its SDG Impact program, the UNDP is also developing best practice impact standards for bond issuers committed to contributing positively to sustainable development and the SDGs.[55] This recently published impact standards cover bond issuers across geography size or sector and includes sovereigns (and sub-sovereigns such as states, provinces, cities, towns or municipalities), supra-nationals and government entities, as well as companies, financial institutions and special purpose entities. The standards aim to provide bond issuers an internal decision-making framework and a benchmark to develop and implement impact strategies aligned to the SDGs and the issuer's organizational strategy. The key elements are listed below:

- contributing positively to sustainable development and achieving the SDGs,

- which cannot be achieved without demonstrating respect for human rights, planetary boundaries and other responsible business practices,

- and is realized through effective impact management and decision-making.

The UNDP SDG Impact initiative will also provide supporting tools and trainings, and envisages developing independent assurance mechanisms in the future.

---

[54] UNESCAP. 2017. *Country Guidance: Public–Private Partnerships for Sustainable Development in Asia and the Pacific*. 1 December.
[55] UNDP. 2021. *SDG Impact Standards. Bond Issuers*.

E. Developing an SDG Bond Framework

There is currently no consensus on what objectives, indicators, or focus areas constitute the core of SDG investment bonds. SDG impact standards do offer some guidance here; they focus on how investments are identified and managed. For potential SDG bond issuers (especially in Asian countries) and SDG investors, the large number of indicators and the need to establish baselines might act as a deterrent to developing SDG bonds. A useful approach for the infrastructure sector could be the development of a simple indicator framework, which might boost momentum for SDG bonds in the region. A generic approach to project level SDG deliverables is presented in Figure 16. It can be used for conceptualizing a project framework and extrapolating this to country level contributions.

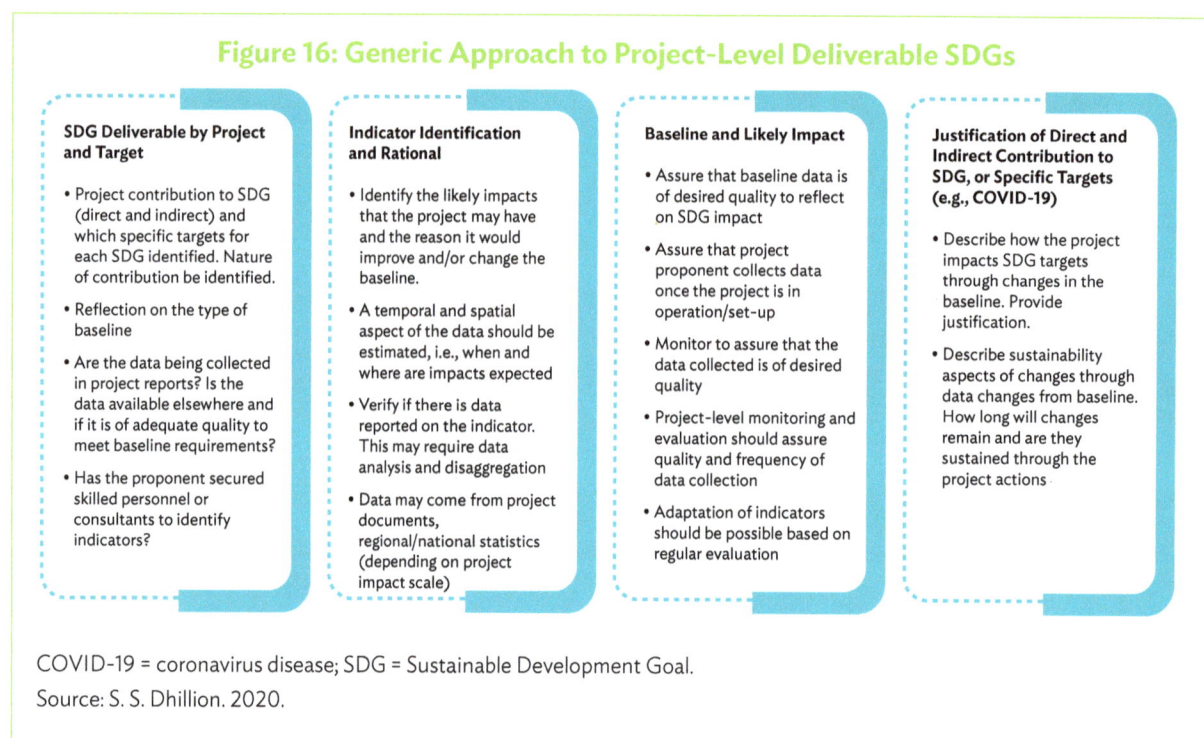

Figure 16: Generic Approach to Project-Level Deliverable SDGs

SDG Deliverable by Project and Target	Indicator Identification and Rational	Baseline and Likely Impact	Justification of Direct and Indirect Contribution to SDG, or Specific Targets (e.g., COVID-19)
• Project contribution to SDG (direct and indirect) and which specific targets for each SDG identified. Nature of contribution be identified. • Reflection on the type of baseline • Are the data being collected in project reports? Is the data available elsewhere and if it is of adequate quality to meet baseline requirements? • Has the proponent secured skilled personnel or consultants to identify indicators?	• Identify the likely impacts that the project may have and the reason it would improve and/or change the baseline. • A temporal and spatial aspect of the data should be estimated, i.e., when and where are impacts expected • Verify if there is data reported on the indicator. This may require data analysis and disaggregation • Data may come from project documents, regional/national statistics (depending on project impact scale)	• Assure that baseline data is of desired quality to reflect on SDG impact • Assure that project proponent collects data once the project is in operation/set-up • Monitor to assure that the data collected is of desired quality • Project-level monitoring and evaluation should assure quality and frequency of data collection • Adaptation of indicators should be possible based on regular evaluation	• Describe how the project impacts SDG targets through changes in the baseline. Provide justification. • Describe sustainability aspects of changes through data changes from baseline. How long will changes remain and are they sustained through the project actions

COVID-19 = coronavirus disease; SDG = Sustainable Development Goal.
Source: S. S. Dhillion. 2020.

To identify SDG deliverables and indicators at project level, the following can be considered when designing an indicator monitoring regime.

(i) **Targets**. Within each of the 17 SDGs are a range of targets that provide the basis for a road map for action. Progress toward these targets is measured through globally harmonized indicators for monitoring performance. At corporate level, the Development Assistance Committee (DAC) of the Organisation for Economic Co-operation and Development (OECD) members and MDB providers that are known to have adopted standard indicator sets and have indicators in the relevant sectors aligned to global SDG indicators, could employ them.[56]

---

[56] Standard indicator sets are defined as a standardized set of indicators used by development cooperation providers to help monitor, that can be used for tiers of results frameworks. Tiers can be (i) development results, (ii) development cooperation results, and (iii) performance information. Standard indicators at Tier 2 typically aggregate project-level results in a way that enables communication of results achieved across multiple projects, countries, and regions. OECD. 2019. *Sustainable Results in Development: Using the SDGs for Shared Results and Impact.* 17 December.

(ii) **Indicators.** It is difficult to select globally applicable and meaningful indicators that may be aligned to a project. The SDGs will have their greatest impact at the local level, so specific project level indicators are unavoidable and necessary. Given that implementation of several goals can provide increments in economic returns, targeted focus on single goals to isolate indicators can be vital to shed light on specific project contributions for each SDG. As indicated, for each project, there are likely to be several goals triggered and thus a range of development indicators will need to be monitored as project indicators.

(iii) **Data.** Ideally, indicators will be based on up-to-date, well-presented, and shareable data that can strengthen decision making, measure progress, and promote accountability of the SDG framework. These should address more general development needs, where possible.

(iv) **Data sources.** Data come from feasibility studies and baseline statistics that form the basis of project impact mitigation, social development, or enhancement measures. These are normally planned when projects are constructed and operated.

(v) **Detailed criteria.** A detailed set of criteria or rules that may be used for identification of indicators are considered to be aligned with the SDGs. This may be particularly important for monitoring and reporting on project performance.

Projects qualifying under a given program must clearly identify the SDG or SDGs that a project addresses and select indicators that will enable impact monitoring in relation to these goals. These indicators should focus on key physical outcomes that can be monitored by technical inspections. In relation to COVID-19 and health, some direct SDG deliverables could be:

- the proportion of households receiving basic services (SDG 3.8.1),
- the proportion of the target population covered by vaccines (SDG 3.b.1),
- the level of health emergency preparedness (SDG 3.d.1),
- the number of beds or working ventilators in a hospital (SDG 3.8.1; SDG 3.d.1),
- the number of students in medical schools (SDG 3.c; SDG 3.b.2; SDG 4.b), and
- the number of people with access to health care (SDG 3.8.1; SDG 3.b.1).

Baselines for indicators would be included in project feasibility studies. Gaps identified during the due diligence process and corrected accordingly will allow for adaptation to focus on tangible indicators. Box 3 shows a 2020 UN framework for a broad socioeconomic response to COVID-19.

Note also that specific subproject indicators may be defined by baseline data and their cumulative values obtained as relevant to direct contributions. For the indirect contribution of baselines to SDG indicators, data may be gauged and evaluated as well. Indirect contributions can go beyond the targeted SDGs, that is to say, other SDGs may be relevant.[57]

An example of a proposed methodology in relation to SDGs for a particular sub-project as part of a larger green infrastructure project is in Appendix 2. Examples of both green and non-green projects are shown. These have been developed based on feedback from specific SDG-related projects underway in Indonesia.

---

[57] For example: (i) SDG 3 (health) related indirect contributions may be to (a) SDG 2.2 (by providing health services (or access) to a larger number of persons (including women and children) and (b) SDG 16.1.3 through increasing chances of detecting features of violence to patients, including children and women; (ii) SDG 5 (gender) can have indirect gender-related contributions through SDG 3 where women are targeted and when gender disaggregated data are collected for indicators for SDG 3 (health) and SDG 4 (education), etc; or (iii) SDG 1.b.1 may have indirect contributions related to pro-poor public social spending and national gender-sensitive development strategies (under which the subproject may fit).

Box 3: Choosing Indicators for COVID-19

When choosing indicators and direct Sustainable Development Goal (SDG) contribution areas, it is important to remember that the coronavirus disease (COVID-19) pandemic has caused an unprecedented global recession with record levels of unemployment. This has created an unparalleled human crisis that is hitting the poorest hardest.

In April 2020, the United Nations (UN) released a framework for the immediate socioeconomic response to COVID-19, as a road map to support countries as they recover socially and economically. It calls for a huge increase in international support to ensure people everywhere have access to essential services and social protection. The socioeconomic response framework consists of the following:

- ensuring that essential health services are still available and protecting health systems;
- helping people cope with adversity, through social protection and basic services;
- protecting jobs, supporting small and medium-sized enterprises, and informal sector workers through economic response and recovery programs;
- ensuring national stimulus packages work for the most vulnerable;
- strengthening multilateral and regional responses; and
- promoting social cohesion and investing in community resilience and response systems.

These UN recommendations also promote environmental sustainability and gender equality with a view to building back better after the pandemic. The UN Secretary-General has stressed that the recovery from the COVID-19 crisis must lead to a different type of economic system. He said the fiscal and monetary policies of the future, along with multilateral responses, need to be large, coordinated, and comprehensive to support the direct provision of resources across the world.

The framework also includes a section showing 10 key indicators for monitoring the human rights implications of COVID-19, many of which are direct SDG deliverables.

Beyond the immediate crisis response, the pandemic should be the impetus to sustain the gains and accelerate implementation of long overdue measures to set the world on a more sustainable development path and make the global economy more resilient to future shocks.

Source: United Nations. 2020. *A UN Framework for the Immediate Socio-Economic Response to COVID-19*. April.

This methodology needs further peer review and is only intended as a draft for discussion that can be modified at the country or project level.

It is important to avoid fragmented or partial reporting of monitoring and evaluation to show performance. It is critical to foster integrated, rather than siloed approaches to data collection and analysis. There is a growing move to design cross-cutting, multifunctional indicators that can provide information and show progress on multiple SDGs or targets, ideally by measuring single data point indicators. But it is vital to ensure there are precise and traceable targets through multiple indicators. Additionally, it is important to assure complete and effective data collection at all stages of a project, including operation and post-project. Where possible, it is recommended to focus on national indicators where appropriate.

Detailed and robust baseline data are essential to successful reporting on performance. Risks associated with securing reliable data sources to build indicators and measure their impact have to be addressed during project conceptualization, feasibility assessment, and implementation.

Villagers collecting drinking water from the community tap next to a 26 cubic meter water reservoir in Nepal. (photo by Gerhard Jörén/ADB)

5 SDG Accelerator Bonds: A New Concept

Many countries have pledged to achieving the SDGs and are at different stages of planning and implementation. A number of ESG instruments, along with SDG bonds, aim to bridge the huge gap in funding required for national projects that will contribute to SDG targets. One of the key challenges is comprehensively linking the SDGs to project outcomes. [58] The SDGs are broad in scope, meaning there is a danger of "SDG washing" where the project needing financing is aligned to one or more of the SDGs in name only with no real sustainable development objective. [59]

Along the lines of green bonds and similar products, there are initiatives to develop a broad frame of reference by which issuers, investors, and bond market participants can evaluate the financing objectives of a given green, social, or sustainability bond program against the SDGs.

This raises the question of how appropriate SDG bonds are, given the challenges associated with them and their perceived similarity with existing thematic bonds. This could be why some governments and multilateral organizations have not followed up after their initial SDG bond offerings and reverted to regular ESG instruments. This reality has also had an impact on mobilizing private finance for SDG-related projects.

The SDG framework, however, can be a powerful tool to link project outcomes when used in a way that encourages synergies and interdisciplinary links. This section presents an overview of the challenges associated with financing the SDGs and examines SDG accelerator bonds, a new instrument that could provide an important addition when developing countries are seeking finance for projects working toward the SDGs.

---

[58] UN Department of Economic and Social Affairs. 2020. How Can Investors Move from Greenwashing to SDG-enabling? *Policy Brief* No. 77. June.
[59] *KPMG*. Reporting the SDGs: How to Get it Right.

A. Challenges to Financing the SDGs

The United Nations Environment Programme (UNEP) estimated in 2017 that nearly $90 trillion is needed globally over the next 15 years to reach the SDGs. Mobilizing finance on this enormous scale means that developing countries need to explore many options simultaneously. These include: internal accruals (tax- and non-tax-based), debt from multilateral and bilateral agencies, private financiers, impact investors, and the public. Accordingly, a range of instruments would need to be made available for different types of investors to participate.

Considerable sums have been raised privately for green projects, with a significant amount of that financing going into renewable energy (Figure 17).[60] But only a small percentage of the capital raised has been for developing countries in other sustainable infrastructure sectors. Often this is due to poor credit ratings and political, economic, and regulatory instability in many low income countries. Although awareness and understanding of the SDGs is quite good among corporates, only a few have concrete strategies for achieving their sustainability goals, indicating a difficulty in translating ideas into real projects.

The sovereigns face a much more daunting task. Many developing countries have relatively weak finances and have to face challenging environmental, social, and governance issues (Box 4). Projects designed to help achieve the SDGs tend to be in the informal sector, in nongovernment organizations, or small and medium-sized enterprises. Not many projects end up being implemented in the large corporate sector. This means that funding requirements need to be met prior to the start of the project and therefore cannot rely on payments based on performance or milestones achieved payments. That is because this group of institutions finds it hard to raise substantial capital for project implementation.

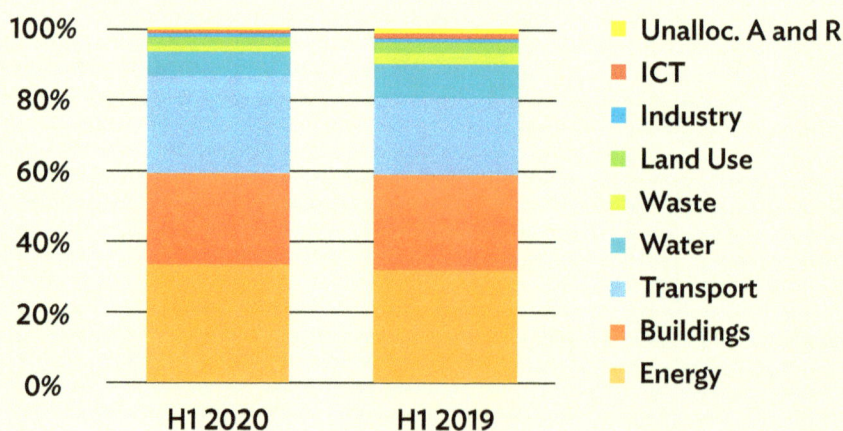

Figure 17: Use of Proceeds First Half, 2020 vs. First Half, 2019 (%)

A and R = adaptation and resilience; H1 = first half of the year; ICT = information and communication technology.
Source: Climate Bonds Initiative. 2020. Climate Bonds Initiative Market Summary H1 2020. August.

[60] Refinitiv. 2020. *Sustainable Finance Review First Half 2020*; CBI. 2020. *Climate Bonds Initiative Market Summary H1 2020.* August.

Box 4: Challenges in Increasing SDG Investment in the ASEAN Region

Some of the challenges ASEAN developing member countries may face in increasing SDG investment are:

- limited integration of SDG principles into infrastructure planning;
- lack of robust bankable project pipelines;
- lack of preparedness of sovereigns for attracting private, institutional, and commercial financiers;
- risk-averse investors with limited capacity to analyze sustainable investments;
- lack of adequate mechanisms to address construction risk that normally deters capital market investors from greenfield projects in developing markets;
- scale and mismatch among projects, market instruments, and institutional investors;
- relatively small investments that would not appeal to large institutional investors;
- lack of suitable aggregation mechanisms along with non-standard projects and cash flow instability;
- lack of coordination when many stakeholders are involved;
- lack of properly functioning bond markets; and
- low credit ratings for potential bond issuers and SDG projects.

ASEAN = Association of Southeast Asian Nations, SDG = Sustainable Development Goal.
Source: Asian Development Bank.

B. Sources of Funding for Sovereigns

With an estimated $90 trillion required, there is an increasing global consensus on the need to substantially increase funding to achieve the SDG targets, along with other institutional, governance, and social reforms to embed sustainable practices. Traditional sources of sovereign funding such as domestic taxes, private savings, and foreign inflows, will continue to be substantial in the near term. But looking further ahead, the enormous anticipated funding gap can only be bridged with access to newer sources of finance, particularly via private, institutional, and commercial (PIC) institutions. The key challenge here is creating an enabling business environment for private capital (savings, foreign direct investment, portfolio investments, remittances, etc.) to flow continuously. A properly coordinated approach that blends traditional sources with concessional finance and PIC funds could accelerate the achievement of the SDGs. Configuring projects with PIC funding, where feasible, could provide the additionality to traditional financing and would result in a deepening of the respective financial markets.

C. The Risk and Return Conundrum for Issuers

SDG, or social, and sustainability bonds are obvious financial instruments that can readily attract private capital for development projects that have impact. However, an emerging challenge in developing countries is the perception of value addition from such bonds. Discussion among member states of the ASEAN about SDG style bonds to date has focused on skepticism about their added value. This is because they would probably be priced the same as any commercial bond, but would entail additional eligibility, indicators, and reporting costs for the issuers.

Where a number of infrastructure projects are not easily bankable and issuing bonds of any kind would be beyond the capacity of potential issuers, these additional costs put an SDG bond product even further out of reach. On the demand side, regular bond investors look for investment opportunities that provide an adequate return for the risks assumed, with SDG related projects in developing countries rarely a priority.

While the number of investors considering sustainable financing (perhaps at a discount on current returns) is increasing, it is unlikely to grow significantly compared with regular investors in the foreseeable future.

In comparison, solid road maps can be identified in green finance and public–private partnership (PPP) approaches. India's Viability Gap Fund for PPPs is an excellent example, as is the ASEAN Catalytic Green Finance Facility (ACGF) for green projects. Both examples show there is now a healthy appetite from project sponsors where a link is clearly demonstrated between concessional finance and project impacts. If such an approach can be developed for SDG bond issuance by state-owned enterprises (SOEs) and local governments (who are responsible for most infrastructure in developing Asia) providing both a big boost in funds and attractive financial terms or concessionality for a project, project entities may well be more likely to consider SDG bonds. Such a structured approach, with commercial returns more likely over the longer term rather than the immediate term, would of course need to appeal to investors.

D. The SDG Accelerator Bond

Keeping the challenges in mind, the concept of an SDG accelerator bond (SAB) is a possible way forward. A SAB makes an explicit template for use in credit enhancement and structuring ideas that are likely already happening in various bonds under development (Figure 18). Naturally, the concept will need to be adapted to local contexts. The main principles underlying the proposed SAB structure include:

(i) **Public sector.** A mechanism envisaged for issuance by governments, SOEs, or special purpose vehicles (SPVs) created for projects by government agencies. PPPs could also be SAB issuers as these are ultimately government concessions (with appropriate mechanisms to ensure that the private partner's investment is not diluted). Focusing on issuance by the public sector addresses the gap in SDG financing from commercial sources to generate product volume and build momentum.

(ii) **Transitional finance.** A SAB is intended as a transitional financing tool for projects that contribute strongly to SDGs that are not already commercially bankable. This may be due to affordability, lack of a tested technical model, or a gradually improving utility structure, but which will gradually see a rise in returns over time if supported. A SAB will be particularly relevant to governments and SOEs who have revenue constraints due to COVID-19, but who are recovering.

(iii) **Improve bankability.** Commercial projects do not need a SAB-type structure. Many SDG projects could raise funds without a bond mechanism at all. A SAB is designed to enable countries to tap into previously constrained flows of funds from potential global investors with a focus on social impact.

(iv) **Catalyze private capital.** A SAB aims to blend traditional market financing with concessional funding from the public sector, whether as credit enhancement guarantees or actual fund flows, under the principle of a risk being taken by the entity best suited to address it. In this regard, initial construction and approval period risks are considered best managed by the public sector and later operations best managed by the private sector.

(v) **Long-term investment.** Returns on a SAB are expected to be prestructured as equivalent to similar market instruments, but over the long term with due incentives and short-term protection for investors to stay in the bond. Investors would be helping a government or SOE make the move into projects that support one or more of the SDGs.

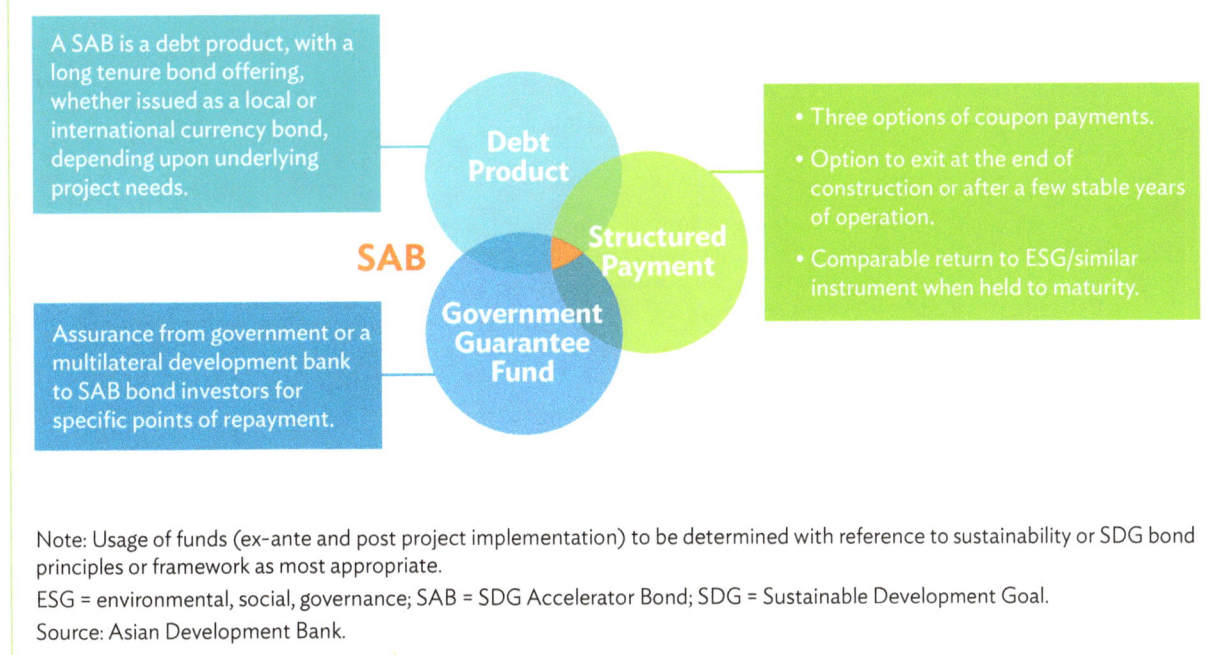

Figure 18: SDG Accelerator Bond Template

A SAB is a debt product, with a long tenure bond offering, whether issued as a local or international currency bond, depending upon underlying project needs.

Debt Product

SAB

Structured Payment

Government Guarantee Fund

- Three options of coupon payments.
- Option to exit at the end of construction or after a few stable years of operation.
- Comparable return to ESG/similar instrument when held to maturity.

Assurance from government or a multilateral development bank to SAB bond investors for specific points of repayment.

Note: Usage of funds (ex-ante and post project implementation) to be determined with reference to sustainability or SDG bond principles or framework as most appropriate.
ESG = environmental, social, governance; SAB = SDG Accelerator Bond; SDG = Sustainable Development Goal.
Source: Asian Development Bank.

Objective

The aim of a SAB is to provide a return comparable to a similar instrument when held to maturity, but offering cheaper funds for projects in initial periods as an incentive to mainstream SDG projects and reach targets more quickly.

Bond and Project Pipelines Preparation

At the outset, it is important to note that SAB development would require supporting both the issuing project entities (development of SDG frameworks, indicators, and targets) and underlying project pipelines to be funded by the bond proceeds. An exercise to accurately gauge investor enthusiasm and commitment would need to be undertaken to assess the sizing and terms of a potential SAB.

SAB Design

Structuring a SAB involves both investors and issuers. An issuer focused on financing their projects may prefer incentive financing or grants that would not align with a bond structure and investor expectations. Equally, a convertible structure whereby initial investment into a project converts into success-based returns or equity can be considered, but the complexity may limit the potential for developing the SDG bond market.

SAB Structure

A SAB is most usefully considered as a debt product, with a long tenure bond offering, whether issued as a local or international currency bond, depending upon underlying project needs (Figure 19). Three possible structures have been developed for a SAB, which would need to be adapted to the local context and investor interest.

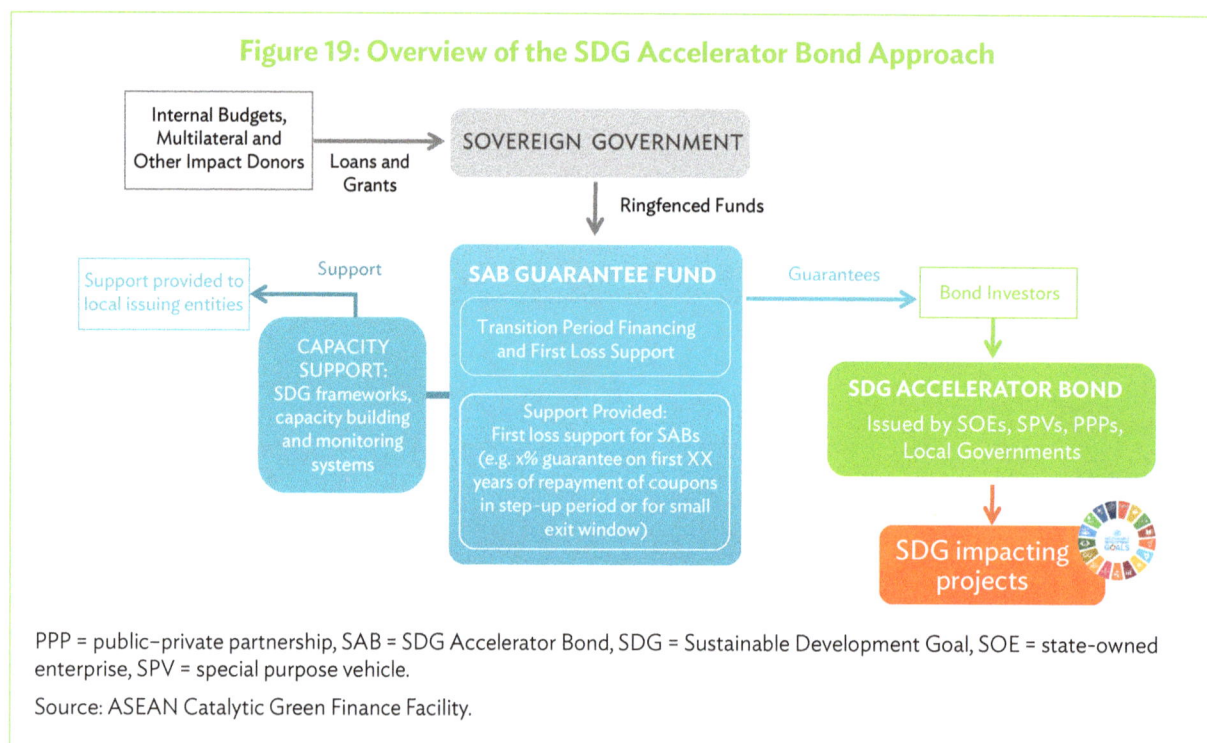

Figure 19: Overview of the SDG Accelerator Bond Approach

PPP = public–private partnership, SAB = SDG Accelerator Bond, SDG = Sustainable Development Goal, SOE = state-owned enterprise, SPV = special purpose vehicle.

Source: ASEAN Catalytic Green Finance Facility.

Payment Options

A SAB may offer three structured payment options:

(i) **Annual market-based returns** for projects that can demonstrate achieving hurdle returns as usually expected by the private investors.

(ii) **Deferred coupon payments**, with yield to maturity in line with comparable ESGs or similar instruments. This would imply that all coupon payments accruing during the construction period of an underlying project in a bond (or a similar period, such as a coronavirus disease [COVID-19] transition period), would not be paid out and deferred for payment. They would be included in a gradually increasing payment flow over the remaining tenor of the bond. Such a structure would help sovereign issuers to endure the early post-COVID-19 period, when revenues are expected to be low. This would better align available cash flows from underlying projects with a staggered bond payment timeline. This deferral would ensure that projects that promote the SDGs are properly funded and included in recovery programs.

(iii) **Zero-coupon payments**, either in the construction or the early stage of operations of underlying projects. This would help alleviate cash flow pressure on projects, particularly in sectors that have been hardest hit by COVID-19, need greater support, and are in danger of being excluded from recovery programs.

Investor Protection Options

To support these bond payment models that are not the usual annual market-based returns, credit enhancement would need to be incorporated.

Exit guarantees are offered to investors through an attached option to the bond, giving a right to sell the bond back to the issuer at a predetermined price at the end of construction or a few stable years of operation.

This could be offered for all three variants, but especially in the deferred and zero-coupon payment options.

The **exit price** for the guarantee above would need to be set at a level which, while providing some upside to investors, should still be lower than if the bond was held to maturity (reaching similar returns to any other bond) to offer an incentive to investors to stay in the bond.

The SDG Accelerator Bond Guarantee Fund

A further proposal is a specific fund developed by a government (with support from MDBs) to provide assurance of SAB bankability to bond investors. The fund would include assurance of payment at specific points, including the exit option points above, perhaps as a first loss guarantee to a project. The guarantee structure can have options to support investor exits at multiple points of time. For instance:

- A guarantee of exit payments (including both coupon and principal) can be provided to the bond holders after construction period or a few years of stable operations. This can be with a lower guaranteed amount, to incentivize investors to stay committed through to the end of the bond tenor.

- A guarantee of a higher value of exit payments at maturity can be provided to investors than those of the exit payments after construction period or a few years of stable operations.

- Other approaches can also be configured depending on the risk perception attached to a specific bond issuance. A typical corporate bond issuance process is attached as Appendix 3. The process for the issuance of a SAB is expected to be along similar lines, with appropriate changes as applicable to sovereigns or SOEs.

Additionally, where required, the fund could also improve the bankability of underlying projects by providing viability gap funds (usually up to 20% of project costs) to support capital expenditure, or by providing revenue top-ups as a credit enhancement mechanism (available to all lenders). All use of funds in these approaches (prior to and post-project implementation) would be linked to clear SDG or sustainability principles embedded and demonstrable at project level.

The guarantee fund will be critical for countries or issuers new to bond issuance. This is especially true post-COVID-19, when global capital might be retreating to safer sectors and wealthier countries. The potential increase in appetite for such a SAB bond with a credit guarantee by an MDB would need to be assessed prior to structuring and issuing, to establish the sizing, credit rating, or the pricing. It is to be noted that typical issuances of ESG bonds or similar market instruments have not depended much on (partial) credit guarantee support mechanisms to attract investor interest.

Indicative Terms of an SDG Accelerator Bond

The indicative terms of a SAB are shown in Table 4 below.

Table 4: Indicative Terms of an SDG Accelerator Bond

Topic	Detail	Additional Comments
Issuer	Respective sovereign or public sector agency.	The SAB could be issued by a sovereign or any national agency (under the line departments responsible for the SDGs/ finance). PPPs, SOEs, and local governments SPVs could also undertake issuance subject to permissible national regulations.
Instrument	SDG accelerator bond secured (x%) zero-coupon fixed or linked to benchmark.	Terminology can be tuned to the SDGs being targeted.

continued on next page

Table 4 continued

Topic	Detail	Additional Comments
Issue size	10% to 20% of the estimated requirement of funds for the SDGs targeted in a specific sector, geographic region, or project, of at least a $100 million bond size to raise interest on global markets.	An estimate of the investment needs of the SDGs would need to be generated. It is envisaged that a SAB would cater to a portion of the total investment requirement of the SDGs being targeted. For an initial pilot SAB, having a clear pipeline of projects would also help in sizing the bond amount correctly.
Target return or yield to maturity	Fixed rate or linked to market benchmarks; comparable to similar ESG bond or market instruments. The returns can also be linked to progress toward the SDGs, provided an objective measurement system is in place prior to issuance.	The yield may match similar ESG instruments over the tenor of the bond. To be determined by the issuer in consultation with the arranger and the second party opinion provider. The rates will be tiered with lower rates at call or put option time, aiming to provide near market returns to the investor during the tenor of the bond.
Guarantor	A government created guarantee fund using funds from government budgets, or multilateral and bilateral development agencies, with clear mechanisms and principles.	The guarantee fund will be critical for countries or issuers new to bond issuance, particularly post-COVID-19, when global capital seeks safer sectors in mature economies.
Security	SDG bonds are secured by a general security interest granted by the issuer against the project assets.	In case the same is being offered, the issuance will be accompanied by the necessary institutional structure.
Financial covenants	The issuer will ensure that the total principal amount of all indebtedness secured is no more than 75% of the project.	Either project level covenants (in addition to the guarantee) if lending to a SOE or PPP, or generalist covenants if used by sovereigns.
Redemption	At par	
Early termination (put)	Investors will have a put option at the end of the construction period or a few years of stable operation, interest paid at x% rate, lower than yield to maturity.	To allow investors to exit at a particular point. The timing could be at the end of construction, or a certain number of years of stable operation. The assurance of coupon and principal repayments could be structured at multiple points, commensurate with the period of investment.
Listing	To be considered by the sovereign.	As an option to the exit provisions, this could provide liquidity and an option for the investors to exit or enter.
Target investors	Pension funds, insurance companies, impact investors, and other financial institutions.	Investors who have the appetite for mid- to long-term tenors, needing moderate returns with lower risk profile. (Not specifically targeted toward those wanting financially superior returns.)
Use of proceeds	The issuer advises that the bond will be verified. The proceeds of the offer are intended to be used to finance projects that contribute to specified SDGs.	An indicative list of projects that contribute to the respective SDGs would be annexed. In addition, an exclusion list would also be provided.
Second party opinion	[Second party] has provided an independent review of the SDG Bonds framework. Following the review, [second party] issued a limited assurance report to the issuer on the proposed use of funds.	Agencies that provide second party opinion, and the framework to be adopted, would need to be agreed upon.

continued on next page

Table 4 continued

Topic	Detail	Additional Comments
Project evaluation and selection	Project eligibility and assessing impact objectives would be carried out in an objective, transparent manner.	A selection and evaluation mechanism would have to be established.
Management of proceeds	The proceeds, along with other contributions by the sovereign and its funders, would be ring-fenced and made available to the selected projects.	A proceeds management mechanism would have to be established.
Reporting	Sustainability reports would be supplied to investors, along with quantitative and qualitative performance indicators, where feasible, in accordance with the requirements of CBI, ICMA.	A reporting mechanism would have to be established.
Other standard provisions	Settlement, conventions, governing law, taxation, and issue logistics.	To be structured based on local regulations.

CBI = Climate Bonds Initiative; COVID-19 = coronavirus disease; ESG = environmental, social, and governance; ICMA = International Capital Market Association; PPP = public–private partnership; SAB = SDG Accelerator Bond; SDG = Sustainable Development Goal; SOE = state-owned enterprise; SPV = special purpose vehicle.

Source: Asian Development Bank.

External Review and Verification

It is proposed that a SAB be verified through a market mechanism of independent external reviews. The process is conducted in advance and consists of an annual post-issuance audit of SAB proceeds, including a review of the SAB's sustainability impact. The SAB process, when dovetailed with infrastructure planning and implementation, is expected to set out indicators that reflect the contribution toward achieving specific SDGs and also to inculcate sustainable practices.

Other Recommendations

- The clear identification of priority SDGs based on nationally agreed commitments is important. Concentrating on just a few SDGs provides better focus, improves investor confidence, and establishes a strong use of funds rationale.

- Prioritizing target projects for which preparatory work has already begun is a good idea.

- Fostering collaboration between stakeholders and encouraging influencers from the government to develop a strong project pipeline to work toward specified SDGs are positive steps.

- The integration of SDG projects into a broader development agenda can enhance coordination and alignment between different stakeholders and sectors of the economy.

- It is good to establish an institutional mechanism for bond issuance. Adopt the principles of the generally accepted SDG framework. Changes to the policy and regulatory environment would be crucial to increasing the appetite for investment on a significant scale.

- Establish a monitoring and reporting framework for continuous performance dissemination to ensure compliance with the basic commitment and to maintain trust among investors.

Sunny Bangchak solar farm in Chaiyabhum Province, Thailand.
(photo by Zen Nuntawinyu/ADB)

6 Building Momentum for the Road Ahead

This publication sets out some of the differences between various types of thematic or ESG bonds, while identifying the unique features of SDG bonds. Examples of SDG bonds issued by subsovereigns, multilateral agencies, financial institutions, and corporates have also been discussed. Challenges to the scaling up of SDG bonds have been identified, as have new concepts, such as the SAB and the SAB guarantee fund. Such approaches might make SDG bonds more attractive, especially in developing Asia where countries are facing the social and economic impact of the COVID-19 aftermath.

A SAB, supported by a guarantee fund, could be a way to rapidly develop pilot bonds in the region. An integrated approach would be needed to develop the ideas in this publication further and some of the key next steps are noted in Figure 20.

SABs may provide an additional way in which developing countries can adopt sustainable practices in their drive to achieve the SDGs, including the following advantages:

- SABs are expected to diversify a group of financial partners while providing leverage to the public funds that are being utilized.

- The deferred initial payments or zero-coupon nature of the bond would alleviate cash flow pressure on the project, particularly in the construction period and the early stage of operations.

- Launching a SAB can trigger a national debate on what is needed to achieve the SDGs and provide inputs to policy making.

- A clear link needs to be established between project outcomes and indicators that demonstrate progress toward the SDGs.

- The SAB process may promote fiscal discipline and better management practices, particularly due to the verification, certification, monitoring, and evaluation required.

- SABs act as one more initiative to deepen capital markets, and steadily move toward aligning with the project's debt features (longer tenors and cheaper pricing).

- This process can assist the respective sovereign to work with MDBs and other partners that drive the development of bankable efforts.

Figure 20: The Road Ahead for SDG Accelerator Bonds

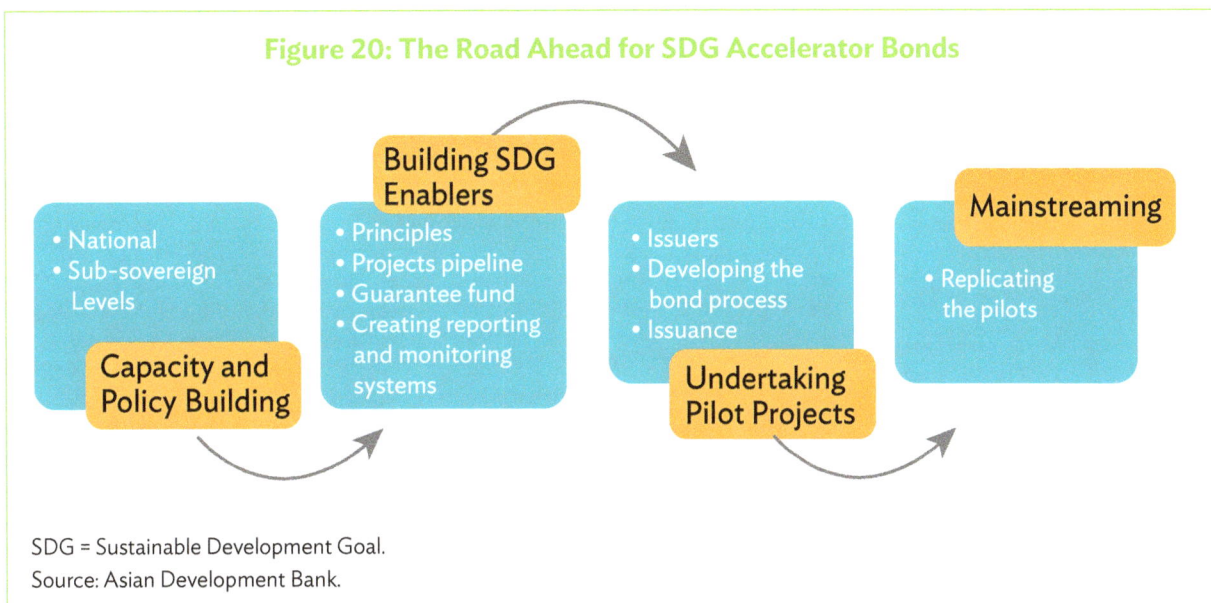

Capacity and Policy Building
- National
- Sub-sovereign Levels

Building SDG Enablers
- Principles
- Projects pipeline
- Guarantee fund
- Creating reporting and monitoring systems

Undertaking Pilot Projects
- Issuers
- Developing the bond process
- Issuance

Mainstreaming
- Replicating the pilots

SDG = Sustainable Development Goal.
Source: Asian Development Bank.

Countries that are interested in developing SDG bonds further, either to fund existing projects or as standalone instruments, should seek appropriate support from MDBs in any of the previously mentioned areas. Working closely at the bond issuer level is critical as the bond structure and risk mitigating guarantees needed will have to be tailored to the local context.

There is a need for countries, projects, and state-owned enterprises to explore SDG bonds as a new source of capital for infrastructure projects in the region. It is particularly the case in this era of financial uncertainty following the COVID-19 pandemic when additional resources are needed to help developing Asia build back better. As a bonus, SDG bonds also provide a framework to stimulate momentum toward meeting the SDGs targets.

Subsovereigns

Issuer	Size	Settlement Date	Tenor (year)	Coupon (%)
Madrid Regional Government (Spain)	€1.25 billion	April 2019	10	1.571

"The Madrid regional government has registered a new benchmark sustainable bond issue with AIAF, BME's Fixed Income market, for an amount of €1.25 billion. This is the fifth sustainable bond issue registered with AIAF by this Public Administration, following those launched since 2016. In this way the Madrid Region becomes an issuer of reference in the field of sustainable finance and AIAF leverages its position as the benchmark market for this type of issues. The bond's individual value is €1,000 and they have a fixed annual interest rate of 1.571%. The final redemption date of the bonds is 30 April 2029. BBVA, HSBC, ING, Banco Sabadell and Banco Santander have acted as Bookrunners. The Madrid regional government has a Baa1 rating, stable outlook, granted by Moody's; BBB +, stable outlook, by S&P and BBB, stable, by Fitch and A-, stable, by DBRS. Gonzalo Gómez Retuerto, Managing Director of BME Renta Fija, stated that *"Green and social bonds have become an asset class in its own right and are highly demanded by international investors."* The total volume issued in 2018 of this type of asset exceeded 167 billion dollars. *"The Spanish issuers rank an outstanding sixth position worldwide"*. BME actively participates in the development of this market through the UN's Sustainable Stocks Exchanges initiative, of which it is a member together with other institutions and global exchanges. The Madrid regional government was the first Spanish Public Administration to launch an issue in the bond market to specifically finance social projects, demonstrating the region's serious commitment about those issues that are not strictly financial, such as climate change and social development."[a]

Similar sustainable bonds have been issued by local Spanish governments including: the Basque government (€500 million, June 2018; €600 million, April 2019) and the city of Barcelona (€35 million, 2017).[b]

AIAF = Asociación Española de Intermediarios Financieros (Spanish Association of Financial Intermediaries); BBVA = Banco Bilbao Vizcaya Argentaria; BME = Bolsas y Mercados Españoles (Stocks and Markets of Spain); BSE = Bono Sostenible Euskadi (Basque Country Sustainable Bond); HSBC = Hongkong and Shanghai Banking Corporation; ING = Internationale Nederlanden Groep; S&P = Standard & Poor's.

[a] BME. 2019. *Madrid Regional Government Registers a New Sustainable Bond Issue in BME.* 14 February.

[b] BME. 2018. *BME Admits to Trading the Basque Government´s New Sustainable Bond.* 12 June; BSE. 2019. *National Councils for Sustainable Development.* Presentation during the Bono Sostenible Euskadi. Basque Country, Spain. 8 July; A. Tejada and J. Romero. 2018. *Green Bonds Continued Breaking Records in 2017.* BBVA. 30 January.

Issuer	Size	Settlement Date	Tenor (year)	Coupon (%)
NRW State (Germany)	€1 billion	18 November 2019	10	0
	€1.5 billion	18 November 2018	20	0.5

"The State of North Rhine-Westphalia issued again a Sustainability Bond in November 2019. Net proceeds finance environmental and social projects of the budgetary year 2019. The bond particularly targets investors focusing on socially responsible investments. [...] The State of North Rhine-Westphalia successfully placed its sixth Sustainability Bond with a total volume of €2.5 billion on the market on November 19, 2019. The bond was issued for the first time in two tranches with different maturities of ten and 20 years."[a]

Similar sustainable bonds have been issued by local German governments including the city of Hanover (€100 million, October 2018).[b]

[a] Nachhaltigkeit. 2019. Sustainability Bond #6 of the State of North Rhine-Westphalia; Helaba. 2019. Federal State of North Rhine-Westphalia 6th Sustainability Benchmark 10 and 20-Year Dual Tranche Transaction Review. 19 November.

[b] Hannover. 2018. Hannovers Green & Social Schuldschein: Nachhaltig Und Gut. 30 October.

Issuer	Size	Settlement Date	Tenor (year)	Coupon
Region Ile-de-France (France)	€500 million	June 2018	15	1.375% OATs+20 bps

Region Ile de France marked its commitment to the socially responsible investment market in 2018 by issuing its sixth green and sustainability benchmark, raising €500 million ($588 million). It priced at the tight-end of the guidance, at OATs+20 basis points, helped by an order book in excess of €1 billion, with more than 60 accounts participating. This 15-year transaction is the longest maturity ever issued by Region Ile de France. Although French buyers snapped up 59% of the paper, it attracted investors from across Europe. The issuer said the quality of its investor base has improved substantially since its first sustainability issue in 2012. Proceeds from the bond have been used to finance eligible projects under the existing green and sustainability bond framework in seven key areas:

- buildings and equipment for education and leisure,
- public transportation and sustainable mobility,
- renewable energy and energy efficiency,
- biodiversity,
- social initiatives aimed at helping vulnerable population groups,
- social housing, and
- economic and socially inclusive development.

Each project financed by the last green and sustainability bond has been analyzed with regards to its positive contribution to the United Nations (UN) Sustainable Development Goals (SDGs). On average, each project contributes positively and directly to 8.5 SDGs.

Each project financed by the last green and sustainability bond has been analyzed with regards to its positive contribution to the UN Sustainable Development Goals (SDGs). On average, each project contributes positively and directly to 8.5 SDGs.

A detailed explanation of the methodology used to scrutinize each project is presented in the reporting. Region Ile de France said it will try to further enhance its impact reporting, by linking the project impacts and the SDGs.[a]

Similar sustainable bonds have been issued by local French governments – including the city of Paris (2017, €320 million).[b]

[a] Environmental Finance. 2019. Sustainability Bond of the Year—Local Authority/ Municipal: Region Ile de France. 2 April; McGlashan, C. 2018. Île-de-France EUR500m 1.375% Jun 33 Green and Sustainability Bond. GlobalCapital. 14 June.

[b] Environmental Finance. 2018. Sustainability Bond of the Year—City of Paris. 28 March.

Issuer	Size	Settlement Date	Tenor (year)	Coupon (%)
Flemish government (Belgium)	€750 million	April 2019	25	1.567
	€500 million	November 2018	15	1.375

In April 2019, the issue of sustainable bonds by the Flemish government was announced. "This is the second time in 6 months that the Flemish Community has issued sustainable bonds. These are bonds, the aim of which is to attract funding for sustainable or social investment. The first bonds' issue in mid-November 2018 raised €500 million from 61 institutional in 11 countries. The interest was even greater this time around with 117 potential investors from 14 countries. A total of €750 million was raised. The bonds run for 25 years and have a yield of 1.567%."[a]

Transaction Summary	
Issuer	Flemish government (Belgium)
Issuer rating	Aa2
Amount	€500 million Reg S only sustainability bond
Maturity date	21 November 2033
Issue/reoffer price	99.009
Coupon	1.375%
Spread at reoffer	19 bps over interpolated OLOs (1.25% April 2033 Green OLO and 3% June 2034 OLO); 97.5 bps over the 5.5% January 2031 Bund
Launched	Monday, 12 November
Payment date	21 November
Joint books	Belfius, Crédit Agricole, KBC, LBBW, Société Générale

Investor Distribution			
By Geography		**By Investor Type**	
France	47.9%	Funds	56.3%
Benelux	32.2%	Insurance/pension funds	32.4%
Germany/Austria	15.3%	Banks	8.7%
Other	4.6%	Other	2.6%

[a] VRT NWS. 2019. Sustainable Bond Issue Raises 750 Million Euro in One Day for the Flemish Exchequer. 9 April; M. Turner. 2019. EIB and Flemish Community Join Fray with ESG Trades. Global Capital. 4 April.

Multilaterals and Bilaterals

Issuer	Size	Settlement Date	Tenor (year)	Coupon (%)
World Bank	Can$1.5 billion	26 July 2019	5	1.80
	€1.5 billion	21 May 2019	10	0.25

On 16 May 2019, the World Bank announced that it had "priced a 10-year Global Sustainable Development Bond, raising EUR 1.5 billion from institutional investors around the globe, to finance its sustainable development activities. This was the World Bank's first 10-year EUR global bond in 10 years, and its first EUR global bond since August 2018 when it issued a 16-year EUR 750 million bond transaction. Barclays, J.P. Morgan, Natixis and TD Securities were the lead managers for the transaction. The bond would be listed on the Luxemburg Stock Exchange and an application will be made to list it on Euronext Dublin. The EUR 1.5 billion global bond was well oversubscribed, with an order book reaching EUR 2 billion with orders from 69 investors. The bond priced with a final spread to the reference Bund of +36.8 basis points."[a]

Transaction Summary	
Issuer	World Bank (International Bank for Reconstruction and Development)
Issuer rating	Aaa/AAA
Amount	€1,500,000,000
Settlement date	21 May 2019
Maturity date	21 May 2029
Issue price	99.577%
Coupon	0.25 % p.a.
Denomination	€1,000
Listing	Luxembourg Stock Exchange; application will be made to be listed on Euronext Dublin
Lead managers	Barclays, JPMorgan Chase & Co., Natixis, TD Securities
ISIN	XS1998930926

Investor Distribution			
By Geography		**By Investor Type**	
Europe	75%	Banks/Bank Treasuries/Corporates	42%
Asia	18%	Central Banks/Official Institutions	32%
Americas	7%	Asset Managers/Insurance/Pension Funds	26%

On 17 July 2019 the World Bank announced that it had "priced the first global benchmark issue of its new fiscal year 2020. The 5-year Global Sustainable Development Bond raised CAD 1.5 billion from institutional investors around the globe to finance World Bank's sustainable development lending. This transaction [matched] the World Bank's largest CAD benchmark, issued in January 2019, the largest bond issued by an SSA (sovereigns, supranational, and agencies) in the Canadian market. BMO Capital Markets, RBC Capital Markets, and TD Securities were joint lead managers for this transaction. The bond [would] be listed on the Luxembourg Stock Exchange. The CAD 1.5 billion offering enjoyed strong market reception from the onset, with indications of interest surpassing CAD1.1 billion overnight. The final orderbook was oversubscribed, with final books in excess of CAD1.85 billion. The high quality, diversified order book was reflected in the allocation to 47 investors globally. This Sustainable Development Bond was issued as part of a World Bank initiative to engage investors on the Sustainable Development Goals (SDGs)."[b]

continued on next page

Table continued

Investor Distribution by Investor Type and Region

Investor Type		Region	
Central Banks/Official Institutions	48%	Europe and Middle East	31%
Asset Managers/Insurance/Pension Funds	29%	Asia	29%
Banks/Bank Treasuries/Corporates	23%	Canada	29%
		US	11

Transaction Summary

Issuer	International Bank for Reconstruction and Development
Issuer rating	Aaa /AAA (Moody's/S&P)
Maturity	5-year
Amount	Can$1.5 billion
Settlement date	26 July 2019
Coupon	1.800% per annum
Coupon payment dates	Payable semi-annually on 26 January and 26 July of each year, beginning on 26 January 2020
Maturity date	26 July 2024
Reference Benchmark	CAN 1.500% due 1 September 2024
Issue price	99.967%
Issue yield	1.807% semi-annually, Actual/Actual
Denomination	Can$1,000 x Can$1,000
Final redemption at maturity (per Specified Denomination)	Par
Spread to Benchmark	CAN 1½ 09/01/24 + 35bps
Listing	Luxembourg Stock Exchange
ISIN	CA459058HA44
Clearing system	CDS, Clearstream, Euroclear
Joint lead managers	BMO Capital Markets, RBC Capital Markets, TD Securities

[a] World Bank. 2019. *World Bank Announces Euro 1.5 Billion 10-year Sustainable Development Bond in Ireland.* 16 May.

[b] World Bank. 2019. *World Bank Kicks Off Fiscal Year with CAD 1.5 Billion Sustainable Development Bond and Highlights the Critical Role of Fresh and Saltwater Resources.* 17 July.

Issuer	Size	Settlement Date	Tenor (year)	Coupon and Price
IDB	Mex$395 million	27 November 2019	3.5	5.64%
	Mex$444 million	27 November 2019	7.0	0%
	£275 million	22 October 2019	7.0	UKT 1.5% 07/22/26 +43 bps
				0.5%
	Can$600 million	10 October 2019	5.0	UKT 1.5% 07/22/26 +43 bps
				1.7%

In September 2019, the Inter-American Development Bank (IDB) announced that it had "priced a new CAD600 million 5-year fixed rate | Sustainable Development Bond ("SDB"). This transaction [represented] the IDB's inaugural SDB issuance, the proceeds of which will be directed to support sustainable development in IDB's member countries aligned with the Bank's strategic priorities to reduce poverty and inequalities in Latin America and the Caribbean by promoting economic and social development in a sustainable, climate friendly way."[a]

In November 2019, the IDB announced that "It issued two new Mex$ deals, 3.5y and 7y respectively under the sustainable development goal (SDG) 13, which promotes climate action. Okasan securities is the distributor of the bond with J.P. Morgan being the sole arranger. With full support from our distributor in Japan, Okasan Securities, the issuance [came] in two parts. One which matures in 3.5 years with fixed coupon payments and the other in seven years which is a zero coupon both funded in Mexican pesos (further details below). The proceeds of the bond will allow IDB to fund its projects in various parts of Latin America and the Caribbean."[b]

Bond Summary Terms	
Issuer	Inter-American Development Bank
Issuer rating	Aaa/AAA
Amount	Can$600 million
Settlement date	10 October 2019
Coupon	1.70 %
Coupon payment dates	Semi-annually on 10 April and 10 October, starting on 10 April 2020 up to and including the Maturity Date
Maturity date	10 October 2024
Issue price	99.824 %
Denominations	Can$1,000
ISIN	CA458182EA63
Listing	London Stock Exchange
Clearing system	CDS, Euroclear, Clearstream
Joint lead managers	RBC Capital Markets, Scotiabank, and TD Securities

In October 2019, the IADB announced that: "It priced a new GBP275 million 7-year fixed rate | Sustainable Development Bond ("SDB"). This transaction is the IDB's second SDB issuance. The new issue carries an annual coupon of 0.500% and will mature on September 15, 2026. It was priced with a spread of 43 basis points over the 1.5% UKT due July 22, 2026. The pricing translates to a semi-annual yield of 0.612%" (footnote a).

continued on next page

Table *continued*

Bond Summary Terms	
Issuer	Inter-American Development Bank
Issuer rating	Aaa/AAA
Amount	£275 million
Settlement date	22 October 2019
Coupon	0.500%
Coupon payment dates	Annually in arrear, with first short coupon on 15 September 2020
Maturity date	15 September 2026
Issue price	99.24%
Denominations	£1,000
ISIN	XS2065728177
Listing	London Stock Exchange
Clearing system	Euroclear, Clearstream
Joint lead managers	Citi, J.P. Morgan, NatWest Markets

Bond Summary Terms	
3.5 years	
Issuer	Inter-American Development Bank
Issuer rating	Aaa/AAA
Amount	Mex$395,000,000
Settlement Date	27 November 2019
Coupon	£5.64%
Coupon Payment dates	Semi-Annually in arrears, on each 25 May and 25 November starting from and including 25 May 2020 to and including the Maturity Date
Issue Price	100.00 %
Maturity Date	25 May 2023
ISIN	XS2069018963

7 years	
Issuer	Inter-American Development Bank
Issuer rating	Aaa/AAA
Amount	Mex$444,000,000
Settlement Date	27 November 2019
Coupon	0%
Issue Price	66.90%
Maturity Date	27 November 2026
ISIN	XS2069018377

[a] IDB. 2019. IDB Launches Inaugural Sustainable Development Bond ("SDB"). 10 October.

[b] IDB. 2019. IDB Issues New Climate Action Sustainable Development Bond with Okasan Securities. 1 November.

Private Sector Financial Institutions

Issuer	Size	Settlement Date	Tenor (year)	Terms
Grupo Bancolombia	COL$657 million	18 June 2019 (approved)	5 10	Private placement. Structured, 100% subscribed, by the Inter-American Development Bank IDB.
Banistmo	$50 million	7 March 2019 (approved)	5	

In March 2019, IDB Invest (a member of the IDB Group) approved the subscription of "the first social gender bond in Latin America, totaling $50 million with a five-year term. Banistmo issued the bond, and IDB Invest [structured] it and [bought] 100 percent of it. The issuance [made] Panama the first country in Latin America with a social bond with a gender focus, aimed exclusively at expanding access to financing for women-led small and medium enterprises. The resources will promote entrepreneurship and women's economic empowerment in that country. [...]The bond [had] a second party opinion from Vigeo Eiris, which accredits compliance with the international social bond standards in The Social Bond Principles of the International Capital Market Association (ICMA). The bond can potentially contribute to four UN Sustainable Development Goals (SDGs): Gender equality (SDG 5), Decent work and economic growth (SDG 8), Industry, innovation and infrastructure (SDG 9) and Reduced inequalities (SDG 10)."[a]

In July 2019, IDB Invest had announced that it had "subscribed a bond in its entirety for 657,000 million Colombian pesos with Grupo Bancolombia. It [was] the first time a private company issues a sustainable bond in Colombia. [The sustainable bond issuance will help finance projects within the Bancolombia portfolio that have a measurable environmental and social benefit, following the international standards established in the Sustainable Bonds Principles. Bancolombia will help contribute up to 10 UN Sustainable Development Goals (SDGs). The framework of this sustainable bond received a second opinion from Vigeo Eiris, an independent third party specialized in these operations."[b]

IDB = Inter-American Development Bank.

[a] IDB. 2019. IDB Issues New Climate Action Sustainable Development Bond with Okasan Securities. 1 November; IDB. 2019. IDB Launches Inaugural Sustainable Development Bond ("SDB"). 30 September.

[b] IDB Invest. 2019. IDB Invest Supports Grupo Bancolombia to Issue the First Sustainable Bond by a Private Company in Colombia. 19 July.

Issuer	Size	Settlement Date	Tenor (year)	Coupon and Price
CaixaBank	$1 billion	September 2019 (announced)	5	mid-swap + 113 bps 0.625%.

In September 2019, CaixaBank announced that "It had become the first Spanish bank to issue a Social Bond to support the Sustainable Development Goals (SDGs) of the United Nations. The company [had] raised 1 billion euros, maturing over 5 years, in the form of non-preferred senior debt, with an objective to facilitate activities that contribute toward economic and social development. Specifically, with this initial issuance, loans are being funded to fight poverty, advocate dignified employment and create jobs in disadvantaged areas of Spain, in line with the United Nations' Sustainable Development Goals. CaixaBank is the only financial institution of the Ibex 35 that has issued bonds like these. The price of the bond [had] been set at 113 basis points over the mid-swap, and the coupon has been established at 0.625%. The success of the issuance [was] reflected in its demand, which amounts to 2.25 billion euros. It will have a rating of Baa3/BBB/BBB+/AL by Moody's, S&P, Fitch and DBRS, respectively. The banks placing this new issuance are ABN, Bank of America ML, Credit Agricole, CaixaBank and HSBC. This August, CaixaBank published the framework for issuing Green, Social and Sustainable Bonds, to support the SDGs of the United Nations, on its corporate website. The framework was verified by Sustainalytics, an expert independent adviser, which affirmed that CaixaBank [had] established a 'credible and high-impact' agenda. The company also carried out a roadshow across different European cities to present this framework to institutional investors."[a]

ABN = Algemene Bank Nederland; DBRS = Dominion Bond Rating Service; HSBC = Hongkong and Shanghai Banking Corporation; S&P = Standard & Poor's.

[a] CaixaBank. 2019. CaixaBank Is the First Spanish Bank to Issue a Social Bond to Support the Sustainable Development Goals (SDGs) of the United Nations. 17 September. Barcelona; D. Wigan. 2019. Caixa Opens Spanish Market for SDG Bonds. The Banker. 1 November.

Issuer	Size	Settlement Date	Tenor (year)	Coupon and Price
ANZ	€1 billion	November 2019 (announced)	10	mid-swap + 140 bps
	€750 million	February 2018 (announced)	5	swap + 15 bps 0.643%

On 22 November 2019, ANZ announced that "It had issued its second Sustainable Development Goals (SDG) Bond in European wholesale debt capital markets, raising €1 billion in Tier 2 capital to fund its lending to sectors such as aged care, education and the environment. The bond is the first Euro SDG Tier 2 bond issued by any bank globally, bringing the total size of ANZ bonds on issue in Green and SDG formats to $A3.4 billion, equivalent. Priced at a spread of 140 basis points over the mid-swap, the 10-year (with a five-year call) bond was heavily oversubscribed, with orders of more than €2.7 billion from more than 150 European and Asian institutional investors". 36% was subscribed by central banks/official institutions, 34% by asset managers, 24% by insurers/pension funds, 6% by banks/financial institutions."[a]

In February 2018, ANZ announced that "It had launched and priced its first Sustainable Development Goals (SDG) bond in the European wholesale debt capital markets, raising €750 million to fund ANZ loans and expenditures that directly promote nine of the United Nations' 17 SDGs. The five-year fixed rate bond was priced at a spread of 15 basis points over the swap rate, with a yield of 0.643%. It was primarily distributed to European institutional investors. ANZ, HSBC, BNP and Barclays acted as Joint Bookrunners on the transaction. The proceeds [were] intended to support projects offering broad social, economic and environmental benefits including funding for hospitals, schools, green buildings, clean water, public transport systems or renewable power plants."[b]

Tenor	5 years
Interest Basis	Fixed Rate
Currency	Euro
Amount	€750 million
Ranking	The bonds are senior medium-term notes
Programme	ANZ's EMTN information memorandum dated 16 May 2017 as supplemented.
Denomination	The bonds will have specified denominations of €100,000 and integral multiples of €1,000 thereafter.
Security Holder Approval	No security holder approval is required in relation to the proposed issue of the bonds
Listing	Application is expected to be made by ANZ for the bonds to be listed on ASX as an ASX wholesale debt listing on or about the issue date.
Clearing	The Notes will not be transferred through, or registered on, the Clearing House Electronic Sub-Register System ("CHESS") operated by ASX Settlement Pty Ltd (ABN 49 008 504 532) and will not be "Approved Financial Products" for the purposes of that system. Interest in the Notes will instead be held in, and transferable through, Euroclear Bank SA/NV or Clearstream Banking S.A.
Selling Restrictions	No transfers will be made to retail clients (as defined in section 761G of the Corporations Act 2001 of Australia) and no bids or offers may be made on an Australian Securities Exchange trading platform with a value less than A$500,000 (or its equivalent in an alternate currency) and as set out in the ANZ's EMTN information memorandum dated 16 May 2017 as supplemented.

ANZ has separately developed Sustainability-Linked Loans (SLLs). Synlait and ANZ signed in September 2019 New Zealand's first SLL (tied to environmental, social, and governance [ESG] metrics). The NZ$50 million 4-year loan "[encouraged] Synlait to further improve its reporting performance against a set of independent ESG criteria." This loan "effectively transfer[s] ANZ's existing $50 million committed 4-year revolver loan into an ESG Linked Loan. A discount or premium to the base lending margin is applied. The performance is based on Sustainalytics' ESG Risk Ratings, an assessment of a company's exposure to financially material ESG risks, measured annually."[c]

continued on next page

Table continued

Incidentally, corporates had previously ventured into the SLL space (irrespective of any SDG reference). "Phillips became the first company to borrow though an SLL in 2017, whose interest on its €1 billion loan was linked to an ESG rating from Sustainalytics, an independent ratings firm. Others followed from a variety of sectors. BNP Paribas-led SLLs include:

- Chemicals. Belgian chemical company Solvay's €2 billion SLL was the first to link to an ambitious greenhouse gas reduction target, in this case one million tonnes of CO_2 by 2025.
- Utilities. Thames Water, a UK utility company, completed a £1.4 [billion] SLL, the first ever corporate to link its borrowing to the GRESB Infrastructure Score, an ESG benchmark for infrastructure assets.
- Hotels and hospitality. Accor Hotels completed a €1.2 billion SLL tied to its Sustainalytics sustainability performance.
- Education. Pearson became the first ever education company to tie its SLL to education targets, such as the number of people educated through their learning programs.
- Housing. L&Q became the first UK housing association to borrow through an SLL linking to employment targets." (BNP Paribas 2019)

ANZ = Australia and New Zealand Banking Group; ASX = Australian Securities Exchange; BNP = Banque Nationale de Paris; CO2 = carbon dioxide; EMTN = Euro Medium Term Note; GRESB = Global Real Estate Sustainability Benchmark; HSBC = Hongkong and Shanghai Banking Corporation; UK = United Kingdom.

[a] S. Klyne. 2019. ANZ Issues €1 Billion Tier 2 SDG Bond. *ANZ Institutional*. 22 November.
[b] P. O'Sullivan. 2018. ANZ Prices First €750m SDG Bond. ANZ.
[c] S. Klyne. 2019. ANZ Issues €1 Billion Tier 2 SDG Bond. *Australia and New Zealand Banking Group Limited (ANZ)*. 22 November.

Corporates

Issuer	Size	Settlement Date	Tenor (year)	Coupon (%)
Starbucks	$1 billion	May 2019 (announced)	5	
	¥85 billion	March 2017 (announced)	7	0.372
	$500 million	May 2016 (announced)	10	2.450

On 13 May 2019, Starbucks announced that "It had completed issuance of a $1 billion Sustainability Bond. It [was] the largest Sustainability Bond the Company [had] issued [until then] and [followed] two previously issued Sustainability Bonds in 2016 and 2017. [...] As with the two previously issued Sustainability Bonds, funds will support ethically sourced coffee." Sustainalytics issued a second party opinion verifying that "the use of proceeds will have positive environmental and social impacts and advance the UN Sustainable Development Goals [SDGs], specifically 1, 8, 9, 11, and 12."[a]

On 17 March 2017, Starbucks announced that "it had closed an underwritten public offering of senior notes, comprising the first global yen-denominated Corporate Sustainability Bond issued in the Japanese market. The company will use the net proceeds from the offering of 85 billion Japanese Yen in 0.372% Senior Notes due 2024 to enhance its sustainability programs around coffee supply chain management through Eligible Sustainability Projects."[b] The issue was underwritten by MUFG and Morgan Stanley, which noted that Starbucks' was "the first-ever Yen sustainability bond by a non-Japanese corporate." Tammy Serbee, Managing Director in Global Capital Markets for Morgan Stanley in New York noted that "[w]ith sustainability becoming a bigger focus in the region following 2015's COP 21 Paris Agreement, we thought it made sense to marry the idea with Starbucks' prior Sustainability Bond framework."[c]

On 16 May 2016, Starbucks announced that it had closed "the first U.S. Corporate Sustainability Bond. The company will use the net proceeds from the offering of $500 million in 2.450% Senior Notes due 2026 to enhance its sustainability programs around coffee supply chain management through Eligible Sustainability Projects."[21] Starbucks then made no specific reference to SDGs.

[a] Starbucks. 2019. Starbucks Completes Issuance of Third and Largest Sustainability Bond. 13 May.
[b] Starbucks. 2017. Starbucks Issues First Global Sustainability Bond in Japan. 17 March.
[c] Morgan Stanley. 2017. Starbucks Debut Yen Bond. 12 April.

Funds and Indexes

In September 2019, Hermes announced that it was launching "high-yield bond funds. The SDG Engagement High Yield Credit Fund will be offered to non-US investors as a Ucits product managed by Hermes Investment Management, and a mutual fund will be available in the US, advised by Hermes affiliate Federated Investment Management, according to a media statement." The fund will invest in companies that are expected to be "SDG leaders in the future, so some may be at the early stages of implementing SDG standards. Hermes had already set up equity funds with so-called SDG 'engagement' and 'impact' themes. The $360 [million] SDG Engagement Equity fund aims to achieve superior financial returns through buying the stocks of companies that are at an early stage of implementing SDG practices within their own operations and in their relationships across their value chains. The high yield credit fund has a similar investment philosophy and strategy. The $240 [million] Hermes Impact Opportunities Equity Fund has a more explicit objective of looking for companies that [aim] to create a positive social or environmental effect through their products or services, and eventually become market leaders in their sectors."[1]

On 27 September 2019, Nomura Securities and Nomura Research Institute announced that "they will publish Nomura-BPI SDGs, a new sub-index to the Nomura Bond Performance Index (NOMURA-BPI). NOMURA-BPI SDGs will select green bonds, social bonds, and sustainability bonds (SDG bonds) from a universe of NOMURA-BPI constituents, as well as calculate the index values and risk indicators. NRI will determine eligibility as SDG bonds based on certain internal rules. The two companies will also provide classification index values and risk indicators such as term to maturity, sector and rating attributions. By developing indices and providing necessary information, NSC and NRI aim to contribute to economic and sustainable social development and promote initiatives to achieve the SDGs, while supporting the growth of the SDG bond market in Japan."[2]

General Purpose SDG Bonds

Issuer	Size		Settlement Date	Tenor (year)	Coupon (%)
Enel	€2.5 billion	T1: €1 billion	October 2019 (announced)	5	0
		T2: €1 billion		8	0.375
		T3: €500 million		15	1.125
	"This bond issue, which will be used to meet the Group's ordinary financial requirements, is linked to Enel's ability to achieve the following Sustainable Development Goals [SDGs]: (i) SDG 7 'Affordable and clean energy,' through the achievement, by December 31st, 2021, of a percentage of installed renewable generation capacity (on a consolidated basis) equal to or greater than 55% of total consolidated installed capacity. As of June 30th, 2019, the figure was already equal to 45.9%; (ii) SDG 13 'Climate action,' through the achievement of a level of greenhouse gas emissions by 2030 equal to or less than 125 g of CO2 per kWh (in 2018 this figure was already equal to 369 g of CO_2 per kWh), in line with the commitment to reduce Enel's direct greenhouse gas emissions per kWh by 70% by 2030 compared to the 2017 values, as certified by the Science Based Targets initiative (SBTi) and consistent with the Paris Agreement on climate change.					

continued on next page

---

1   R. Walker. 2019. Hermes Launches SDG High Yield Bond Funds. Fund Selector Asia. 27 September.
2   Nomura Research Institute. 2019. Nomura Announces Launch of Joint Research on Nomura-BPI SDG Bonds. 17 April

Table continued

Issuer	Size	Settlement Date	Tenor (year)	Coupon (%)
	The interest rate [for the first 2 tranches] will remain unchanged to maturity subject to achievement of the sustainability target indicated under point i. above as of December 31st, 2021. [I]f that target is not achieved, a step-up mechanism will be applied, increasing the rate by 25 bps as of the first interest period subsequent to the publication of the auditor's assurance report. The interest rate for the last tranche will remain unchanged to maturity subject to achievement of the sustainability target indicated under point ii. above as of December 31st, 2030. If that target is not achieved, a step-up mechanism will be applied, increasing the rate by 25 bps as of the first interest period subsequent to the publication of the report issued by a third-party expert charged with validating the methodology for measuring CO2 emissions applied by the Group."[a]			
	$1.5 billion	10 September 2019	5	2.650
	"The interest rate will remain unchanged to maturity subject to achievement of pre-defined sustainability targets (being a percentage of installed renewable generation capacity (on a consolidated basis) equal to or greater than 55% of total consolidated installed capacity) as of 31 December 2021. If that target is not achieved, a step-up mechanism will be applied, increasing the rate by 25 bps starting from the first interest period subsequent to the publication of the assurance report of the auditor engaged for this purpose."[b]			

On 10 October 2019 "Enel launched a multi-tranche 'sustainable' bond for institutional investors on the European market totaling 2.5 billion euros. The bond is linked to the achievement of the United Nations Sustainable Development Goals (SDGs) and is the Group's first 'General Purpose SDG Linked Bond' issued on the European market. The bond, which [was] guaranteed by Enel and launched as part of Enel and EFI's medium-term bond issue programme (Euro Medium Term Notes Programme - EMTN), was almost four times oversubscribed, with total orders of about 10 billion euros and the significant participation by Socially Responsible Investors (SRIs), enabling the Enel Group to continue to diversify its investor base. The issue is listed on the Irish Stock Exchange." Enel obtained "a discount of around 10 bps with respect to a comparable issue without sustainability characteristics, representing a discount of around 20% across the weighted average cost of the whole transaction."

This bond issue, "which will be used to meet the Group's ordinary financial requirements, [was] linked to Enel's ability to achieve the following Sustainable Development Goals:

(i) SDG 7 'Affordable and clean energy,' through the achievement, by December 31st, 2021, of a percentage of installed renewable generation capacity (on a consolidated basis) equal to or greater than 55% of total consolidated installed capacity. As of June 30th, 2019, the figure was already equal to 45.9%;

(ii) SDG 13 'Climate action,' through the achievement of a level of greenhouse gas emissions by 2030 equal to or less than 125 g of CO_2 per kWh (in 2018 this figure was already equal to 369 g of CO_2 per kWh), in line with the commitment to reduce Enel's direct greenhouse gas emissions per kWh by 70% by 2030 compared to the 2017 values, as certified by the Science Based Targets initiative (SBTi) and consistent with the Paris Agreement on climate change."

"The interest rate for the first 2 tranches will remain unchanged to maturity subject to achievement of the sustainability target indicated under point i. above as of December 31st, 2021. If that target is not achieved, a step-up mechanism will be applied, increasing the rate by 25 bps as of the first interest period subsequent to the publication of the auditor's assurance report."

The interest rate for the last tranche "will remain unchanged to maturity subject to achievement of the sustainability target indicated under point ii. above as of December 31st, 2030. If that target is not achieved, a step-up mechanism will be applied, increasing the rate by 25 bps as of the first interest period subsequent to the publication of the report issued by a third-party expert charged with validating the methodology for measuring CO_2 emissions applied by the Group."

continued on next page

Table continued

Issuer	Size	Settlement Date	Tenor (year)	Coupon (%)

More specifically, the issue was structured in the following tranches:

Tranche 1: 1B euros at a fixed rate of 0.00%, maturing 17 June 2024 and linked to SDG 7 "Affordable and clean energy:"
- "the issue price was set at 99.123% and the effective yield at maturity equal to 0.189%;
- the interest rate will remain unchanged to maturity subject to achievement of the sustainability target indicated above as of 31 December 2021;
- if that target is not achieved, a step-up mechanism will be applied, increasing the rate by 25 bps as of the first interest period subsequent to the publication of the auditor's assurance report."

Tranche 2: 1B euros at a fixed rate of 0.375 %, maturing 17 June 2027 and linked to SDG 7 "Affordable and clean energy:"
- "the issue price was set at 99.257 % and the effective yield at maturity equal to 0.474%
- the interest rate will remain unchanged to maturity subject to achievement of the sustainability target indicated above as of 31 December 2021;
- if that target is not achieved, a step-up mechanism will be applied, increasing the rate by 25 bps as of the first interest period subsequent to the publication of the auditor's assurance report."

Tranche 3: 500M euros at a fixed rate of 1.125 %, maturing 17 October 2034 and linked to SDG 13 "Climate action:"
- "the issue price was set at 98.922% and the effective yield at maturity is equal to 1.204%;
- the interest rate will remain unchanged to maturity subject to achievement of the sustainability target indicated above as of 31 December 2030;
- if that target is not achieved, a step-up mechanism will be applied, increasing the rate by 25 bps as of the first interest period subsequent to the publication of the report issued by a third-party expert charged with validating the methodology for measuring CO2 emissions applied by the Group."[a]

On 8 September 2019, Enel had already launched the world's first "SDG bonds," "a single-tranche 'sustainable' bond for institutional investors on the US and international markets totaling 1.5B US$ (1.4B euro). The issue, guaranteed by Enel, was oversubscribed by almost three times, with total orders of approximately 4 billion US dollars and the significant participation of Socially Responsible Investors (SRI), allowing the Enel Group to continue to diversify its investor base. This bond issue, the first of its kind and intended to meet the Company's ordinary financing needs, [was] linked to the Group's ability to achieve, by 31 December 2021, a percentage of installed renewable generation capacity (on a consolidated basis) equal to or greater than 55% of total consolidated installed capacity. To ensure the transparency of the results, the achievement of that target (as of 30 June 2019, the figure was already equal to 45.9%) will be verified by a specific assurance report issued by the auditor engaged for this purpose. The operation has been structured as a single tranche issue of 1.5B US dollars paying a rate of 2.650% maturing 10 September 2024. The issue price has been set at 99.879% and the effective yield at maturity is equal to 2.676 %. The settlement date for the issue is 10 September 2019. The interest rate will remain unchanged to maturity subject to achievement of the sustainability target indicated above as of 31 December 2021. If that target is not achieved, a step-up mechanism will be applied, increasing the rate by 25 bps starting from the first interest period subsequent to the publication of the assurance report of the auditor."[c]

bps = basis points, CO_2 = carbon dioxide, EFI = Enel Finance International N.V., g = gram, kWh = kilowatt-hour.

[a] Enel. 2019. Enel Successfully Places its First General Purpose SDG Linked Bond on the European Market. 16 October.

[b] Enel. 2019. Enel Launches the World's First "General Purpose SDG Linked Bond", Successfully Placing a 1.5 Billion U.S. Dollar Bond on the U.S. Market. 6 September.

[c] Energynomics. 2019. ENEL launches the world's first "sdg bonds", placing 1.5 bln. USD. 9 September.

Issuer	Size	Settlement Date	Tenor (year)	Coupon (%)
World Bank	$ 3.52 million	14 December 2018	5	0

On 17 December 2018, the World Bank announced that in a series of similar bond issues across regions it had "priced new bonds that offer retail investors in [Hong Kong, China] and Singapore the opportunity to promote the Sustainable Development Goals (SDGs). Returns on the bond are linked to an equity index that tracks the performance of companies advancing global development priorities set out in the SDGs, including climate, gender, and health. This [marked] the first time that the World Bank has offered SDG index-linked bonds to retail investors in Asia. The return on investment in the bonds is directly linked to the stock performance of companies included in the Selective Sustainable Development Goals World MV Index. The index tracks 30 companies that, based on the methodology developed by Vigeo Eiris' Equities, dedicate at least one fifth of their activities to sustainable products, or are recognized leaders in their industries on socially and environmentally sustainable issues. Solactive applies volatility and diversification filters to reach the final index composition. Vigeo Eiris is a global provider of environmental, social and governance research to investors and public and private corporates. Previously, the World Bank [had] issued SDG index-linked bonds in Belgium and Switzerland, with another offering currently underway in Australia. The World Bank will use the proceeds to support the financing of projects that advance its goals of eliminating extreme poverty and boosting shared prosperity, and that are aligned with the SDGs. The issuance builds on growing demand from institutional and retail investors for high quality, liquid assets that promote social impact. The five-year bonds raised US$3.52 million."[a]

Issuer	International Bank for Reconstruction and Development, IBRD
Issuer rating	Aaa /AAA (Moody's / S&P)
Issuance amount	$3,520,000
Settlement date	14 December 2018
Maturity	5 years
Index	Solactive Sustainable Development Goals World MV Index (SOLWGOAL)
Coupon	None
Maturity date	14 December 2023
Issue price	100%
Specified Denomination	$10,000
Final redemption at maturity (per Specified Denomination)	Specified Denomination plus any Index Linked Interest Amount
Index Linked Interest Amount	The product of $10,000 multiplied by the Participation Rate multiplied by the greater of (i) the Final Index Return and (ii) zero (0)
	Final Index Return = the quotient, expressed as a percentage, as calculated by the Calculation Agent, equal to (i) the Final Index Level (closing level of the Index on 30 November 2023) minus the Initial Index Level (closing level of the Index on 3 December 2018) divided by (ii) the Initial Index Level
	Participation Rate = 165%
Listing	None
ISIN	XS1896850929
Clearing system	Euroclear, Clearstream
Sole lead manager	BNP Paribas

[a] World Bank. 2018. World Bank Introduces Sustainable Development Goals Index-Linked Bonds for Retail Investors in Hong Kong and Singapore. 17 December.

Examples of SDG Accounting in ADB SDG Indonesia One–Green Finance Facility Project in Indonesia

Methodology to Measure SDG Impact of Subprojects

The preliminary subproject assessment will establish the key Sustainable Development Goals (SDGs) that the subproject addresses. The next step, to be undertaken by the consultants for the subproject sponsor, is to select indicators that will enable monitoring of the impact of the subproject on these goals. As the Green Finance Facility (GFF) is under the SDG Indonesia One (SIO) umbrella, it is important to also nominate the SDGs that the project addresses and can deliver (Tables A1 and A2 have information for green and non-green subprojects). Suggested indicators for judging SDG performance can be extracted from the global indicator framework for the SDGs and targets of the 2030 Agenda for Sustainable Development developed by the United Nations (United Nations 2017).

These indicators should focus on key physical outcomes of the infrastructure subprojects that can be monitored by engineering inspection in periodic reviews of the subproject. Flexibility should be assessed at the onset for the potential adaptation needs of indicators and their range. The generic process is as follows for a particular SDG:

(i) Identify the key physical indicator(s) that can provide a measure of SDG impact. For example, in relation to SDG 6 "Ensure availability and sustainable management of water and sanitation for all," indicators such as "increase in % of households with 24-7 water supply in house" should be used.

(ii) PT Sarana Multi Infrastruktur, Persero (PT SMI) should identify key physical indicators that are linked to achieving SDG benefits and pro-rata physical achievement to benefit achievement. Thus, building water treatment for 50% of the design population will achieve 50% of total benefit at a given time. If only 40% of the population are actually covered by that scheduled time then achieved adaptation benefit will be 20% less than calculated for that scheduled time (all other things being equal).

(iii) As is the case here, the basic concept used in respect of assessing sustainability and impact is to establish, for the particular project in the particular sector, current baseline performance. In this case, this baseline is the practice of the current operation of the particular subproject. However, this performance should be compared to current best national and/or international practice.

(iv) As above, these calculations should be provided by the consultants for the project sponsor or, if the sponsor is incapable of contracting such consultants, by subproject development consultants procured by PTSMI.

In respect of all these assessments, the methodology used for calculating the values used should also be carefully documented and provided to PT SMI so that the values and underlying assumptions may be validated during the review process.

The format for the assessment and reporting, including SDG-related indicators, is set out in Tables A1.1 and A1.2, both for green and non-green subprojects.[3]

Table A2.1: Project Assessment and Reporting for Green Subprojects and Related SDG Impacts

Taxonomy Assessment		Component Assessments				Total % of Green Components	Assessment Justification Notes by Component Initial Assessment/Updates as Needed			
		1	2	3	4					
	% Invest	30%	30%	40%						
							1	2	3	4
Nominate taxonomy sector, area and sub-area per component (may be more than one per component)										
Investment Criterion/ Subcriterion/Base Indicator		Component Assessments				Totals	Project Assessment Notes/Achievement by Component Initial Assessment/Updates as Needed			
		1	2	3	4					
Impact										
Total GHG emission savings (TCO$_2$e project life)										
Total adaptation beneficiaries—direct and indirect (project life)										
Resource Efficiency Assessment		Component Assessments					Project Assessment Notes/Achievement by Component Initial Assessment/Updates as Needed			
		1	2	3	4					
Impact							1	2	3	4
Nominate Indicator per component										
SDG Assessment		Component Assessments					Project Assessment Notes/Achievement by Component Initial Assessment/Updates as Needed			
		1	2	3	4					
Impact							1	2	3	4
Nominate SDGs addressed per component (may be more than one per component)										

GHG = greenhouse gas, tCO$_2$e = ton of carbon dioxide equivalent, SDG = Sustainable Development Goal.
Source: Asian Development Bank.

---

[3] This was prepared by M. Lindfield for the overall Green Framework of the ADB SDG Indonesia One – Green Finance Facility project, and adapted by the authors; ADB. 2020. Project Concept Paper. Proposed Loan and Technical Assistance Grant Indonesia: Sustainable Development Goals Indonesia One – Green Finance Facility Phase 1. Manila.

Table A2.2: Project Assessment and Reporting for Non-Green Subprojects with SDG Impact

		Example
Subproject	Project description. What is the objective? Outputs?	New vaccination center established in public hospital serving XXX people, including YYY medical personnel and ZZZ type of equipment in a designated or expected spatial area of coverage.
Likely SDG delivered	Does the project contribute to one or more of the SDG? List SDG/s and nature of direct contribution	SDG 3: Ensure healthy lives and promote well-being for all at all ages
Target	List targets for identified SDG/s	3.b Support the research and development of vaccines and medicines for the communicable and non-communicable diseases that primarily affect developing countries, provide access to affordable essential medicines and vaccines, in accordance with the Doha Declaration on the TRIPS Agreement and Public Health, which affirms the right of developing countries to use to the full the provisions in the Agreement on Trade-Related Aspects of Intellectual Property Rights regarding flexibilities to protect public health, and, in particular, provide access to medicines for all.
Potential indicator (for data available)	List of physical indicators to measure the project impact, provided by project reports	3.b.1 Proportion of the population with access to affordable medicines and vaccines on a sustainable basis.
Rationale for selected indicator	Describe	Better access to vaccines improves people's health, reduces public and private medical expenses related to diseases, improves worker and student productivity, etc.
Baselines	Establish baseline for every indicator	X% of the population with access to vaccines before the center was established, and if relevant, within a designated spatial area. Area for which the new center is expected to provide coverage to, if relevant.
Impact of the project	Describe how the project will improve the baseline	Y% of the population within the designated area with access to vaccines. YY% of the population outside the designated spatial area availed of the center and thus had access to vaccines.
Justify impact on sectors affected by COVID-19 and its recovery	Describe	Healthier population will be more resilient to potential new pandemics. Presence of center will act as contributing to preparedness for potential pandemic like needs.
Proposed: Indirect contribution to other SDGs	List SDG/s and nature of indirect contribution	Healthier population will be more productive (at work and school), having an indirect impact on SDGs 4 and 8.

COVID-19 = coronavirus disease, SDG = Sustainable Development Goal.
Source: Asian Development Bank.

The process to issue corporate bonds will consist of the following steps:

(i) A company wanting to issue a corporate bond turns to an arranger, generally a securities broker or bank, for assistance with structuring the bond and raising capital. The arranger usually handles both parts. The legal process and the raising of capital often take longer the first time a company carries out a bond issue. This is because a more thorough review of the company (due diligence) has to be carried out and because the company is often unknown to the market. The legal information is accompanied by an investor presentation in which the issuer (the borrower) presents its business strategy, financial status, and prospects. The issuer then undertakes to report its accounts on a continuous basis.

(ii) Corporate bonds can be registered on a stock exchange but are rarely traded electronically. Instead, bonds are usually traded over the counter and generally over the phone. The arranger is responsible for maintaining a secondary market for the bond. The bond's payments are made via a clearing house. Most corporate bonds have an agent to represent the interests of the bondholders.

(iii) To increase transparency throughout the securities market, a new directive came into effect in the European Union (EU) on 3 January 2018: MiFID II. This regulatory framework means, for example, that the price and volume must be registered with the local financial supervisory authority the day after a transaction has taken place (Jool Academy 2020).

Figure A3.1: The Issuance Process of Corporate Bonds

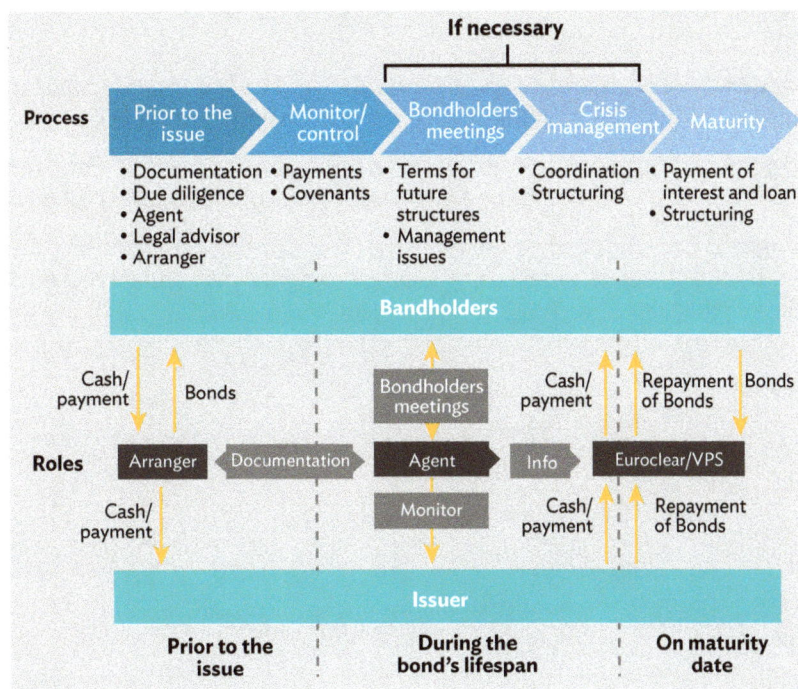

VPS = Verdipapirsentralen ASA.
Source: Jool Academy. What Is a Corporate Bond?

(iv) The issuer appoints the relevant parties for the transaction. These include:

- **Lawyers.** The issuer and lead manager instruct lawyers to draft the documents (usually the lead manager's lawyers), comment on the drafts and prepare the legal opinions.

- **Lead manager and managers.** A financial institution usually arranges the entire transaction, including the sale of the bonds, legal documentation and settlement procedures. This is the lead manager. It then contacts other financial institutions (called managers) to form a syndicate that agrees to buy the bonds to sell to investors.

- **Paying agents.** Paying agents are financial institutions that act as the agents of the issuer in making payments of interest and principal to the bondholders throughout the life of the bonds.

- **Trustee (or fiscal agent).** A bond issue usually has either a trustee or a fiscal agent. There is never both a trustee and a fiscal agent. A fiscal agent acts for the issuer as a principal paying agent while a trustee acts on behalf of the bondholders as an intermediary between them and the issuer.

- **Printers.** Specialist financial printers may need to be instructed to print the prospectus and, if applicable, the definitive bonds.

- **Auditors.** The issuer's (and, if applicable, guarantor's) auditors need to be informed of the bond issue and provide comfort letters to the managers at signing and closing.

Other parties may also need to be appointed depending on the type of bond issue. For example:

- **Registrar.** For registered bonds only. A financial institution that maintains a register of the names and addresses of registered bond owners and any change in ownership when bonds are sold.

- **Transfer agent.** For registered bonds only. A financial institution that maintains a record of the names and addresses of registered bond owners and any change in ownership when bonds are sold.

- **Calculation agent.** A financial institution that makes certain calculations under a debt security. This is usually only required to calculate floating rates of interest on a floating rate note or in a complex transaction involving derivatives.

- **Listing agent.** For bonds listed on a stock exchange. The listing agent advises the issuer on the procedure for listing and submits the documents for listing to the relevant stock exchange.

- **Rating agent.** An agency (such as Fitch, Moody's, or Standard & Poor's) that assesses the financial position and creditworthiness of an issuer and assigns a rating to its bond issue.

- **Process agent.** Only required where the issuer is a non-United Kingdom [UK] issuer. An agent appointed by the issuer to receive any legal documents that are served on the issuer in legal proceedings in the UK.

References

The Asset. 2018. Asean Launches Social and Sustainability Bond Standards. 16 October. https://www.theasset.com/capital-markets/35200/asean-launches-social-and-sustainability-bond-standards.

Association of Southeast Asian Nations (ASEAN) Capital Markets Forum (ACMF). 2018. *ASEAN Green Bond Standards*. October. https://www.theacmf.org/images/downloads/pdf/AGBS2018.pdf.

———. 2018. *ASEAN Social Bond Standards*. October. https://www.theacmf.org/images/downloads/pdf/ASBS2018.pdf.

———. 2018. *ASEAN Sustainability Bond Standards*. October. https://www.theacmf.org/images/downloads/pdf/ASUS2018.pdf.

Asian Development Bank (ADB). 2017. *Meeting Asia's Infrastructure Needs*. Manila. https://www.adb.org/publications/asia-infrastructure-needs.

———. 2018. Strategy 2030: Achieving a Prosperous, Inclusive, Resilient, and Sustainable Asia and the Pacific. Manila. https://www.adb.org/documents/strategy-2030-prosperous-inclusive-resilient-sustainable-asia-pacific.

———. 2020. 2019 Development Effectiveness Review: Scorecard and Related Information. April 2020. https://www.adb.org/documents/development-effectiveness-review-2019-report.

———. 2020. Project Concept Paper. Proposed Loan and Technical Assistance Grant Indonesia: Sustainable Development Goals Indonesia One – Green Finance Facility Phase 1. Manila. https://www.adb.org/sites/default/files/project-documents/54152/54152-001-cp-en.pdf.

———. 2020. ADB Supports Thailand's Green, Social, and Sustainability Bonds for COVID-19 Recovery. 24 September. https://www.adb.org/news/adb-supports-thailand-green-social-and-sustainability-bonds-covid-19-recovery.

———.2021. ADB's Support for the Sustainable Development Goals: Enabling the 2030 Agenda for Sustainable Development through Strategy 2030. March 2021. https://www.adb.org/documents/adb-support-sdgs-2030-agenda.

Avery, H. 2016. CSR Bonds: Are Sustainability Bonds Better than Green? *Euromoney*. 23 September. https://www.euromoney.com/article/b12kq32709kvlz/csr-bonds-are-sustainability-bonds-better-than-green?copyrightInfo=true.

BFSI.com. 2020. Sustainable Bond Issuance Hits Record High in Q2 as Social Bonds Surge: Moody's. 17 August. https://bfsi.economictimes.indiatimes.com/news/industry/sustainable-bond-issuance-hits-record-high-in-q2-as-social-bonds-surge-moodys/77592378.

BME. 2018. BME Admits to Trading the Basque Government´s New Sustainable Bond. 12 June. https://www.bolsasymercados.es/ing/Media/Press-Release/20180612/nota_20180612_2/BME_admits_to_trading_the_Basque_Government_s_new_sustainable_bond.

———. 2019. Madrid Regional Government Registers a New Sustainable Bond Issue in BME. 14 February. https://www.bolsasymercados.es/ing/Media/Press-Release/20190214/nota_20190214_4/Madrid_regional_government_registers_a_new_sustainable_bond_issue_in_BME.

BNP Paribas. 2019. Sustainable Finance: The Rise and Rise of Sustainability-Linked Loans. 23 July. https://cib.bnpparibas.com/sustain/sustainable-finance-the-rise-and-rise-of-sustainability-linked-loans_a-3-3008.html.

Bono Sostenible Euskadi. 2019. National Councils for Sustainable Development. Presentation during the Bono Sostenible Euskadi. Basque Country, Spain. 8 July. https://stakeholderforum.org/wp-content/uploads/2019/06/Session-4-No.-1-Jorge-Fernandez-Basque-Government-Sustainability-Bond.pdf.

CaixaBank. 2019. CaixaBank Is the First Spanish Bank to Issue a Social Bond to Support the Sustainable Development Goals (SDGs) of the United Nations. Barcelona. 17 September. https://www.caixabank.com/comunicacion/noticia/caixabank-is-the-first-spanish-bank-to-issue-a-social-bond-to-support-the-sustainable-development-goals-sdgs-of-the-united-nations_en.html?id=41906.

Center for Global Development, Development Impact Bond Working Group. 2013. *Investing in Social Outcomes: Development Impact Bonds*. 7 October. https://www.cgdev.org/publication/investing-social-outcomes-development-impact-bonds.

Chance, C. 2019. *From Junk Bonds to Just Bonds: The Increasing Importance of ESG Financing In European High Yield. Clifford Chance.* London. https://www.cliffordchance.com/content/dam/cliffordchance/briefings/2019/07/from-junk-bonds-to-just-bonds-the-increasing-importance-of-esg-financing-in-european-high-yield.pdf.

CISION PR Newswire. 2019. IDB Invest and Banistmo Announce First Gender Bond in Latin America. 2 August. https://www.prnewswire.com/news-releases/idb-invest-and-banistmo-announce-first-gender-bond-in-latin-america-300895795.html.

Climate Bonds Initiative (CBI). Basic Certification. https://www.climatebonds.net/certification/get-certified.

———. 2018. *Green Bonds as a Bridge to the SDGs*. Climate Bonds Initiative Briefing Paper. June. https://www.climatebonds.net/2018/06/green-bonds-bridge-sdgs-focus-sdg-6-7-9-11-13-15.

———. 2019. *Green Bonds Market H1 2019*. July. https://www.climatebonds.net/files/reports/h1_2019_highlights_final.pdf

———. 2019. *Climate Bonds Taxonomy*. October. https://www.climatebonds.net/files/files/CBI_Taxonomy_Tables-Nov19.pdf.

———. 2020. *2019 Green Bond Market Summary*. February. https://www.climatebonds.net/system/tdf/reports/2019_annual_highlights-final.pdf?file=1&type=node&id=46731&force=0.

———. 2020. *Climate Bonds Initiative Market Summary H1 2020*. August. https://www.climatebonds.net/resources/reports/green-bonds-market-summary-h1-2020.

———. 2021. *Green Bond Pricing in the Primary Market: July–December 2020*. March. https://www.climatebonds.net/resources/reports/green-bond-pricing-primary-market-h2-2020.

———. 2021. *Sustainable Debt: Global State of the Market 2020*. April. https://www.climatebonds.net/resources/reports/sustainable-debt-global-state-market-2020.

———. 2021. *ASEAN Sustainable Finance State of the Market 2020*. April. https://www.climatebonds.net/resources/reports/asean-sustainable-finance-state-market-2020.

Dhillion, S. S. 2020. SDG screening and potential indicators for projects. https://www.tofnorway.org/who-we-are/.

Enel. 2019. Enel Launches the World's First "General Purpose SDG Linked Bond", Successfully Placing a 1.5 Billion U.S. Dollar Bond on the U.S. Market. 6 September. https://www.enel.com/content/dam/enel-common/press/en/2019-September/SDG%20bond%20ENG%20(003).pdf.

———. 2019. Enel Successfully Places its First General Purpose SDG Linked Bond on the European Market. 16 October. https://www.enelrussia.ru/en/media/news/d201910-enel-successfully-places-its-first-general-purpose-sdg-linked-bond-on-the-european-market-with-a-multi-tranche-issue-of-25-billion-euros.html#:~:text=SDG%207%20%E2%80%9CAffordable%20and%20clean%20energy%E2%80%80.

Energynomics. 2019. ENEL Launches the World's First "SDG Bonds", Placing 1.5 bln. USD. 9 September. http://www.energynomics.ro/en/enel-launches-the-worlds-first-sdg-bonds-placing-1-5-bln-usd/.

Environmental Finance. 2018. Sustainability Bond of the Year—City of Paris. 28 March. https://www.environmental-finance.com/content/awards/green-bond-awards-2018/winners/sustainability-bond-of-the-year-city-of-paris.html.

———. 2019. Sustainability Bond of the Year—Local Authority/ Municipal: Region Ile de France. 2 April. https://www.environmental-finance.com/content/awards/green-social-and-sustainability-bond-awards-2019/winners/sustainability-bond-of-the-year-local-authority/-municipal-region-ile-de-france.html.

Global Commission on Adaptation. 2019. Adapt Now: A Global Call for Leadership on Climate Resilience. 13 September. https://gca.org/reports/adapt-now-a-global-call-for-leadership-on-climate-resilience/.

The Global Commission on the Economy and Climate. 2018. *Unlocking the Inclusive Growth Story of the 21st Century: Accelerating Climate Action in Urgent Times—Key Findings and Executive Summary.* https://newclimateeconomy.report/2018/wp-content/uploads/sites/6/2018/09/NCE_2018Report_ExecutiveSummary.pdf.

Gore, G. 2019. Update 1-Enel Ditches Green Bonds for Controversial New Format. 4 October. *Reuters*. https://www.reuters.com/article/enel-ditches-green-bonds-for-controversi-idUSL5N26O403.

Gourc, A. 2019. Social Bonds: The Next Frontier for ESG Investors. *BNP Paribas*. 23 July. https://cib.bnpparibas.com/sustain/social-bonds-the-next-frontier-for-esg-investors_a-3-3005.html.

Government of Thailand. 2020. Sustainability Bond Issuance: Investor Presentation. July. https://www.pdmo.go.th/pdmomedia/documents/2020/Jul/01 Project Emerald_investor roadshow presentation v upload.pdf.

Government of the United States, Department of Commerce, National Oceanic and Atmospheric Administration. 2020. Ocean Acidification. https://www.noaa.gov/education/resource-collections/ocean-coasts/ocean-acidification.

Hannover. 2018. Hannovers Green & Social Schuldschein: Nachhaltig Und Gut. 30 October. https://www.hannover.de/Service/Presse-Medien/Landeshauptstadt-Hannover/Meldungsarchiv-für-das-Jahr-2018/Hannovers-Green-Social-Schuldschein-Nachhaltig-und-gut.

Helaba. 2019. Federal State of North Rhine-Westphalia: 6th Sustainability Benchmark10 and 20 Year Dual Tranche Transaction Review. 19 November. https://www.nachhaltigkeit.nrw.de/fileadmin/download/Nachhaltigkeitsanleihe/Transaction_Review_NRW_Sustainable_Dual_Tranche_Nov_2019.pdf.

International Capital Market Association (ICMA). Resource Centre. https://www.icmagroup.org/green-social-and-sustainability-bonds/resource-centre/.

———. 2020. ICMA. Green, Social and Sustainability Bonds: A High-Level Mapping to the SustainableDevelopment Goals. June. https://www.icmagroup.org/assets/documents/Regulatory/Green-Bonds/June-2020/Mapping-SDGs-to-Green-Social-and-Sustainability-Bonds-2020-June-2020-090620.pdf.

———. 2020. *Climate Transition Finance Handbook 2020*. December. https://www.icmagroup.org/sustainable-finance/the-principles-guidelines-and-handbooks/climate-transition-finance-handbook/.

Inter-American Development Bank (IDB). 2019. IDB Launches Inaugural Sustainable Development Bond ("SDB"). 30 September. https://www.iadb.org/en/news/idb-launches-inaugural-sustainable-development-bond-sdb.

———. 2019. IDB Launches Inaugural GBP Sustainable Development Bond ("SDB"). 10 October. https://www.iadb.org/en/news/idb-launches-inaugural-gbp-sustainable-development-bond-sdb.

———. 2019. IDB Issues New Climate Action Sustainable Development Bond with Okasan Securities. 1 November. https://www.iadb.org/en/news/idb-issues-new-climate-action-sustainable-development-bond-okasan-securities.

IDB Invest. 2019. Banistmo Social Bond with a Gender Focus. https://www.idbinvest.org/en/projects/banistmo-social-bond-gender-focus.

———. 2019. IDB Invest Supports Grupo Bancolombia to Issue the First Sustainable Bond by a Private Company in Colombia. 19 July. https://www.idbinvest.org/en/news-media/idb-invest-supports-grupo-bancolombia-issue-first-sustainable-bond-private-company.

International Finance Review (IFR). 2019. Borrowers respond to bondholder demand on ESG standards. 23 May. https://www.ifre.com/story/1588162/borrowers-respond-to-bondholder-demand-on-esg-standards-vfgdpdcqqd.

International Labour Organization (ILO). 2020. ILO: As Job Losses Escalate, Nearly Half of Global Workforce at Risk of Losing Livelihoods. 29 April. https://www.ilo.org/global/about-the-ilo/newsroom/news/WCMS_743036/lang--en/index.htm.

———. 2020. COVID-19 leads to massive labour income losses worldwide. 23 September. https://www.ilo.org/global/about-the-ilo/newsroom/news/WCMS_755875/lang--en/index.htm.

Jool Academy. What Is a Corporate Bond? https://joolgroup.com/jool-academy-what-is-a-corporate-bond/.

JPMorgan Chase & Co. 2019. *Environmental Social and Governance Report 2019*. https://impact.jpmorganchase.com/content/dam/jpmc/jpmorgan-chase-and-co/documents/jpmc-cr-esg-report-2019.pdf.

KPMG. Reporting the SDGs: How to Get it Right. https://home.kpmg/xx/en/home/insights/2020/01/reporting-sdgs-how-to-get-it-right.html.

Klyne, S. 2019. ANZ Issues €1 Billion Tier 2 SDG Bond. Australia and New Zealand Banking Group Limited (ANZ). *ANZ Institutional*. 22 November. https://institutional.anz.com/insight-and-research/November/anz-issues-billion-tier-2-SDG-bond.

Mary, S., C. Schuetz, and O. A. Albrecht. 2019. SDG Bonds: Their Time Has Come. *PIMCO*. 28 October. https://global.pimco.com/en-gbl/insights/viewpoints/sdg-bonds-their-time-has-come.

Mahler, D. G. et al. 2020. "Updated Estimates of the Impact of COVID-19 on Global Poverty." Data Blog. World Bank Blog. 8 June. https://blogs.worldbank.org/opendata/updated-estimates-impact-covid-19-global-poverty.

McGlashan, C. 2018. Île-de-France EUR500m 1.375% Jun 33 Green and Sustainability Bond. GlobalCapital. 14 June. https://www.globalcapital.com/article/b18n17dkyn6rrr/206ledefrance-eur500m-1375-jun-33-green-and-sustainability-bond.

Morgan Stanley. 2017. Starbucks Debut Yen Bond. 12 April. https://www.morganstanley.com/ideas/starbucks-sustainability-bond-sustainable-investing.

Mullin, K. 2017. Capital Markets: How to Build a Social Bond Market. *Euromoney*. 18 September. https://www.euromoney.com/article/b14sxhkbb0047d/capital-markets-how-to-build-a-social-bond-market.

Mutua, D. C. 2020. Social Debt Surges to Record as Borrowers Tackle Coronavirus. *Bloomberg*. 29 July. https://www.bloomberg.com/news/articles/2020-07-29/social-debt-surges-to-record-as-borrowers-tackle-coronavirus.

Nachhaltigkeit. 2019. Sustainability Bond #6 of the State of North Rhine-Westphalia. https://www.nachhaltigkeit.nrw.de/projekte/nachhaltigkeitsanleihen/sustainability-bond-6/.

Noh, H. J. 2018. Financial Strategy to Accelerate Green Growth. *ADBI Working Paper Series* No. 866. Tokyo: Asian Development Bank Institute. https://www.adb.org/publications/financial-strategy-accelerate-green-growth.

Nomura Research Institute. 2019. Nomura Announces Launch of of Joint Research on Nomura-BPI SDG Bonds.17 April. https://www.nomuraholdings.com/news/nr/nsc/20190417/20190417.pdf.

Organisation for Economic Co-operation and Development (OECD). 2019. *Sustainable Results in Development: Using the SDGs for Shared Results and Impact*. 17 December. https://www.oecd.org/publications/sustainable-results-in-development-368cf8b4-en.htm.

O'Sullivan, P. 2018. ANZ Prices First €750m SDG Bond. *ANZ*. https://institutional.anz.com/insight-and-research/ANZ-Prices-First-750m-SDG-Bond.

Poh, J. 2019. ESG Debt: A User's Guide to Ever-Growing Menu of Bonds And Loans. *Bloomberg*. 16 October. https://www.bloomberg.com/news/articles/2019-10-16/esg-debt-a-user-s-guide-to-ever-growing-menu-of-bonds-and-loans.

Thomson Reuters Practical Law. Practical Law. Bond Issues: Step-by-Step Guide. https://uk.practicallaw.thomsonreuters.com/1-505-0428?transitionType=Default&contextData=(sc. Default)&firstPage=true.

Refinitiv. 2020. Sustainable Finance Review First Half 2020. https://www.refinitiv.com/perspectives/market-insights/refinitiv-analyzes-the-sustainable-finance-market/.

Robinson-Tillett, S. 2020. Survey: What words and phrases would you banish from sustainable finance discussions? Responsible Investor. 1 June. https://www.responsible-investor.com/articles/survey-what-words-and-phrases-would-you-banish-from-sustainable-finance-discussions.

Sachs, J., et al. 2020. *Sustainable Development Report 2020: The Sustainable Development Goals and COVID-19*. Cambridge: Cambridge University Press. June. https://www.sdgindex.org/reports/sustainable-development-report-2020/

Shrof, C. and D. Constantin. 2015. Corporate Social Responsibility: An Asian Perspective. *Conventus Law*. 13 August. http://www.conventuslaw.com/report/corporate-social-responsibility-an-asian/.

Starbucks. 2016. Starbucks Issues the First Corporate Sustainability Bond. 16 May. https://stories.starbucks.com/press/2016/starbucks-issues-the-first-u-s-corporate-sustainability-bond/.

———. 2017. Starbucks Issues First Global Sustainability Bond in Japan. 17 March. https://stories.starbucks.com/press/2017/starbucks-offers-its-first-sustainability-bond-in-japan/.

———. 2019. Starbucks Completes Issuance of Third and Largest Sustainability Bond. 13 May. https://stories.starbucks.com/press/2019/starbucks-completes-issuance-of-third-and-largest-sustainability-bond/.

Susantono B., Alisjahbana A., and Wignaraja K. 2020. A Determined Path to SDGs in 2030, Despite COVID-19 Pandemic. ADB. 20 August. https://www.adb.org/news/op-ed/determined-path-sdgs-2030-despite-covid-19-pandemic-bambang-susantono-armida-salsiah.

Sustainable Development Investment Partnership. Country Financing Roadmaps. http://sdiponline.org/country-financing-roadmaps.

Synlait. 2019. Synlait Secures New Zealand's First ESG Linked Loan. 23 September. https://www.synlait.com/news/synlait-secures-new-zealands-first-esg-linked-loan/.

Tejada, A. and J. Romero. 2018. Green Bonds Continued Breaking Records in 2017. *BBVA*. 30 January. https://www.bbva.com/en/green-bonds-continued-breaking-records-2017/.

Toole, M. 2021. Sustainable Finance Continues Surge in Q1. *Refinitiv*. 23 April. https://www.refinitiv.com/perspectives/future-of-investing-trading/sustainable-finance-continues-surge-in-q1/.

Turner, M. 2019. EIB and Flemish Community Join Fray with ESG Trades. *Global Capital*. 4 April. https://www.globalcapital.com/article/b1dtxg83t3dwky/eib-and-flemish-community-join-fray-with-esg-trades.

United Nations. SDG Indicators. https://unstats.un.org/sdgs/indicators/indicators-list/.

———. 2015. Sustainable Development Goals and Targets. https://www.un.org/sustainabledevelopment/sustainable-development-goals/.

———. 2020. High-Level Event on Financing for Development in the Era of COVID-19 and Beyond. Initiative on Financing for Development in the Era of COVID-19 and Beyond. https://www.un.org/en/coronavirus/financing-development.

———. 2020. A UN Framework for the Immediate Socio-Economic Response to COVID-19. April. https://unsdg.un.org/sites/default/files/2020-04/UN-framework-for-the-immediate-socio-economic-response-to-COVID-19.pdf.

United Nations Conference on Trade and Development. 2014. World Investment Report. Investing in the SDGs: An Action Plan.New York: United Nations. https://unctad.org/system/files/official-document/wir2014_en.pdf.

United Nations Department of Economic and Social Affairs. 2020. How Can Investors Move from Greenwashing to SDG-enabling? *Policy Brief* No. 77. June. https://www.un.org/development/desa/dpad/wp-content/uploads/sites/45/publication/PB_77.pdf.

United Nations Development Programme. 2017. Financing the Sustainable Development Goals in ASEAN. 16 November. https://asean.org/wp-content/uploads/2012/05/Report-on-Financing-SDGs-in-ASEAN1.pdf.

———. 2020. *SDG Impact Standards for Bonds*. https://sdgimpact.undp.org/assets/SDG-Impact-Standards-for-Bonds_First-Public-Consultation-Draft.pdf.

———. 2021. SDG Impact Standards. Bond Issuers. https://sdgimpact.undp.org/assets/Bond-Issuers-Standards_1.0.pdf.

United Nations Environment Programme. 2016. *Green Bonds: Country Experiences, Barriers and Options*. http://unepinquiry.org/wp-content/uploads/2016/09/6_Green_Bonds_Country_Experiences_Barriers_and_Options.pdf.

———. 2017. High-Level SDG Financing Lab. 18 April. https://unepinquiry.org/event/high-level-sdg-financing-lab/.

United Nations Economic and Social Commission for Asia and the Pacific. 2017. Country Guidance: Public–Private Partnerships for Sustainable Development in Asia and the Pacific. 1 December. https://www.unescap.org/resources/country-guidance-public-private-partnerships-sustainable-development-asia-and-pacific.

United Nations Educational, Scientific and Cultural Organization. Global Education Coalition for COVID-19 Response. https://en.unesco.org/covid19/educationresponse/globalcoalition.

United Nations Framework Convention on Climate Change. 2017. Human Health and Adaptation: Understanding Climate Impacts on Health and Opportunities for Action. Synthesis Report by the Secretariat. Subsidiary Body for Scientific and Technological Advice 46th Session. Bonn. 8–18 May. https://unfccc.int/sites/default/files/resource/docs/2017/sbsta/eng/02.pdf.

United Nations Sustainable Development Goals. Financing for Sustainable Development. https://www.un.org/sustainabledevelopment/financing-for-development/.

———. High-Level Political Forum on Sustainable Development. https://sustainabledevelopment.un.org/hlpf.

VRT NWS. 2019. Sustainable Bond Issue Raises 750 Million Euro in One Day for the Flemish Exchequer. 9 April. https://www.vrt.be/vrtnws/en/2019/04/09/sustainable-bond-issue-raises-750-million-euro-in-one-day-for-th/.

Walker, R. 2019. Hermes Launches SDG High Yield Bond Funds. *Fund Selector Asia*. 27 September. https://fundselectorasia.com/hermes-launches-sdg-high-yield-bond-funds/.

Wigan, D. 2019. Caixa Opens Spanish Market for SDG Bonds. *The Banker*. 1 November. https://www.thebanker.com/Markets/Issuers/Caixa-opens-Spanish-market-for-SDG-bonds?ct=true.

World Bank. 2018. World Bank Introduces Sustainable Development Goals Index-Linked Bonds for Retail Investors in Hong Kong and Singapore. 17 December. https://www.worldbank.org/en/news/press-release/2018/12/17/world-bank-introduces-sustainable-development-goals-index-linked-bonds-for-retail-investors-in-hong-kong-and-singapore.

———. 2019. World Bank Announces Euro 1.5 Billion 10-Year Sustainable Development Bond in Ireland. 16 May. https://www.worldbank.org/en/news/press-release/2019/05/16/world-bank-announces-euro-15-billion-10-year-sustainable-development-bond-in-ireland.

———. 2019. World Bank Kicks Off Fiscal Year with CAD 1.5 Billion Sustainable Development Bond and Highlights the Critical Role of Fresh and Saltwater Resources. 17 July. https://www.worldbank.org/en/news/press-release/2019/07/17/world-bank-kicks-off-fiscal-year-with-cad-1-5-billion-sustainable-development-bond-and-highlights-the-critical-role-of-fresh-and-saltwater-resources.

World Health Organization. 2018. Climate Change and Health. 1 February. https://www.who.int/news-room/fact-sheets/detail/climate-change-and-health.